D0672140

138 Quick Ideas to Get More Clients

Howard L. Shenson
Jerry R. Wilson

WAGGONER LIBRARY
TREVECCA NAZARENE UNIVERSITY

WAGGONER LIBRARY
DISCARD

John Wiley & Sons, Inc.
New York • Chichester • Brisbane • Toronto • Singapore

This text is printed on acid-free paper.

Copyright © 1993 by John Wiley & Sons, Inc.

All rights reserved. Published simultaneously in Canada.

Reproduction or translation of any part of this work beyond that permitted by Section 107 or 108 of the 1976 United States Copyright Act without the permission of the copyright owner is unlawful. Requests for permission or further information should be addressed to the Permissions Department, John Wiley & Sons, Inc.

This publication is designed to provide accurate and authoritative information in regard to the subject matter covered. It is sold with the understanding that the publisher is not engaged in rendering legal, accounting, or other professional services. If legal advice or other expert assistance is required, the services of a competent professional person should be sought. *From a Declaration of Principles jointly adopted by a Committee of the American Bar Association and a Committee of Publishers.*

Library of Congress Cataloging-in-Publication Data

Shenson, Howard L.
138 quick ideas to get more clients/Howard Shenson, Jerry Wilson.
p. cm.
Includes indexes.
ISBN 0-471-58952-7 (cloth : alk. paper). — ISBN 0-471-58951.9 (pbk. : alk. paper)
1. Business consultants—Vocational guidance—United States. 2. Professions—United States—Marketing. I. Wilson, Jerry R., 1944- . II. Title. III. One hundred and thirty eight quick ideas to get more clients.
HD69.C6S515 1993
001'.068'8—dc20 93-19576

Printed in the United States of America

10 9 8 7 6 5 4 3 2

Publisher's Note

Howard L. Shenson had completed a first draft of the manuscript for this book when he died unexpectedly. We at John Wiley & Sons regret the untimely passing of a valued author, colleague, and friend.

Although Mr. Shenson was uniquely qualified to write this book because of his extensive consulting experience, we at John Wiley—together with Mr. Shenson's literary agent, Jeff Herman—were able to find a distinguished co-author to complete Mr. Shenson's work. Jerry R. Wilson is an internationally known consultant, speaker, and author of *Word-of-Mouth Marketing.* Jerry Wilson stepped in to complete and perfect *138 Quick Ideas to Get More Clients.*

John Wiley & Sons is proud to offer the finished book to Howard Shenson's many admirers the world over.

Contents

Foreword

Few consultant/authors have had an impact on the profession of consulting to management as strong as that of Howard L. Shenson, CMC. During his tenure as a professional consultant, Howard Shenson counseled more than 500 clients, including Fortune 100 firms, small businesses, not-for-profit entities, individual corporate executives, and consultants with professional practices. The author of over a dozen books, he was also the publisher of his own nationally recognized newsletter. His seminars on establishing a successful consulting practice were attended by over 150,000 would-be consultants and those with established practices. Howard's works have been the subject of more than 700 magazine and newspaper articles. He was truly a "giant" in setting the pace for those of us in the practice of consulting to management.

Howard passed away in November 1992. I had the privilege of knowing Howard as both a friend and a peer for over 20 years. In 1990, in my capacity as Chairman of the National Bureau of Professional Management Consultants, I asked Howard to become involved in identifying and developing the Common Body of Knowledge for the consulting profession. The majority of his recommendations were accepted. In June 1992, the National Bureau published the Common Body of Knowledge. This document is the foundation for a proposed national certification program for professional consultants to management and is subject to proposed legislative certification.

In reviewing the manuscript of one of Howard's latest writings, *138 Quick Ideas to Get More Clients*, I expected and did see the clear-cut concepts that made Howard famous. He was able to get to the core of a subject, and the reader rapidly gained knowledge from a practical viewpoint. My own research proves that

Howard Shenson wrote more on the subject of professional consulting than any other consultant/author.

My compliments, also, to Jerry Wilson, who was able to complete the contents for this publication. Having been in the profession of consulting for nearly 30 years, I can recommend this new book, *138 Quick Ideas to Get More Clients*, as a learning resource for developing additional clients quickly.

Vito Tanzi
Chairman, National Bureau of Professional Management Consultants

Acknowledgments

My special thanks to our National Coordinator, JoAnn Mann, for her extra effort with the typing, organizing, and editing of this book.

Introduction

Why not face facts. You can be the most terrific speaker, consultant, attorney, engineer, or professional the world has ever seen, but to really succeed, you must successfully *sell your services*. You must generate leads and convert them into paying clients. And some dramatic market changes mean you must also "rethink" your sales and marketing strategies.

While the market for professional services continues to grow, so does the number of firms and individuals competing for that business. In other words, to really succeed means to differentiate yourself from others.

This book will help you add dozens of "bite size" strategies to your existing marketing efforts. From marketing your services consistently and on a regular basis to networking productively and getting media exposure, you can differentiate yourself again and again.

Perhaps the "ideal" way to differentiate yourself is to continue the big or major differentiators you already use, then systematically add these 138 quick ideas as soon as you can.

With the current downsizing of hundreds of America's corporations, thousands of professionals are being thrown out of work. Many of these white-collar professionals are finding speaking, consulting, and professional services a lucrative alternative when traditional employment isn't available. This influx of qualified professionals means an explosion of competition for you. It means you must continue to enhance your marketing efforts.

Getting Started . . . How to Use These 138 Strategies

This book exists for one reason . . . to help you better market your services and make more money! Ideally you need all the clients you can serve. And you want to be paid hefty professional fees most only dream of. Starting now.

First, as you read these sales and marketing strategies, note that most are "bite size" or stand-alone strategies you can implement *right now*. You won't need to rewrite your marketing plan or hire seven more people to use them.

Second, have a fluorescent highlighter, colored felt-tip pen or such in hand as you read. Not every strategy will appeal to you. Look for "Aha's!"—as in "Aha . . . this is a good idea I can use." Mark it up! Write in notes and thoughts about how you will use it. Jot down how you will modify or adapt the strategy to your existing marketing plan. You may even want to write instructions to a secretary or assistant right in the book.

Third, as you begin seeing results from implementing these strategies, think how you can improve, modify, and make them more effective. *Challenge yourself* to be a marketing innovator.

Fourth, mark some strategies as possibilities for future use. Then make a note in your Day-Timer©, tickler, or appointment book to review this book on a periodic basis—perhaps once each quarter. This book won't make you a dime gathering dust on your credenza!

Fifth, *don't quit!* All too often, professionals market like crazy until they get busy, then they let their marketing effort slip away. The secret of the pros is consistency, consistency, consistency.

In your hands is the secret weapon that you need to compete more effectively. Best of all, every one of these 138 strategies has been tested and proven by the authors and their professional colleagues. These ideas work!

Got your pen? Get started . . . .

Jerry R. Wilson, CSP

Jerry Wilson is an internationally known professional speaker. For information on his innovative sales and customer service topics for a convention, conference or sales meeting, call Jerry Wilson at 1(800)428-5666 or (317)257-6876; or write to Jerry Wilson and Associates, P.O. Box 55182, Indianapolis, IN 46205.

Chapter 1

Marketing Do's

1. Market Your Services on a Regular Basis

Devote about 15 to 25% of your working hours to marketing and selling. The time to market is *not* when you have run out of clients. Market on a regular and consistent basis. Most professionals prefer to spend their time doing creative and technical work. They find all kinds of "creative avoidance"—excuses to put off and avoid marketing and selling. They will tell you that they are too busy taking care of clients or doing research. Successful professionals recognize that acquiring business is just as important as serving clients.

If Wednesday is marketing day, then Wednesday must only be spent on marketing—regardless of the demands that clients make. Professionals who market consistently can enjoy higher incomes than those who market only when they run out of clients.

If you have difficulty finding time to market while serving clients on a timely basis, then it is time to expand your services by hiring an assistant or by developing subcontractor relationships that can help you.

2. Market Only to Decision Makers

Pre-qualify prospects by asking them if they are in a position to make a commitment for your services—provided, of course, you can demonstrate a cost-efficient method for solving their problem. Don't be hesitant to insist that you meet directly with the decision makers. Spending time with guards to the palace gate can be wasteful. You also can't depend upon these people to present your ideas correctly. Remember, kings meet only with kings.

3. Market to Every Member of a Decision-Making Committee

When selling to committees, take time to talk to each individual involved in the decision making. Listen to each person's concerns. Presell each decision maker in terms of those concerns. When meeting with the committee as a whole, demonstrate how you are providing adequate balance to ensure that each concern is met.

If a governing board is responsible for making a decision to do business with you, be sure to obtain an invitation to attend the board meeting in which your association or contract will be discussed. Prompt the staff member who handles the agenda items. Indicate that the meeting is significant to you and that you need to be present. The board would prefer to talk to you and you will have the opportunity to sell yourself. Don't rely on someone else to communicate your important message.

4. Make Selling Your Services Your Number One Job

Most professionals love the work they do and the services they provide. However, all too many dislike or even despise the selling process required to make their business work.

If your professional practice requires you to be a salesperson, then resolve this "reluctant astronaut" issue today. Here's how:

1. Write a new job description for yourself and list sales and marketing as your most important task. Make it Job One! (Ever try to do great work without a client to serve?)
2. Start using positive self talk, such as, "I'm a great salesperson, and I enjoy selling my services." Successful selling starts with the right attitude.
3. Do what successful sales representatives do. Attend sales classes and seminars, read sales magazines, invest in audio and video sales training, and network with other sales pros.
4. Pretend you work for someone else. Set up goals, deadlines, quotas, and most important, rewards. It is critical to motivate yourself to do the sales activities that will bring your results. And as you succeed as a salesperson, allow yourself some liberal rewards—including time off.

5. Stack Up the Value

Consultants, speakers, and professionals often spend untold hours on work that is necessary but not directly billable. Most clients are unaware of the required groundwork. Such preparation time is intangible and difficult for clients to appreciate in terms of dollars. Periodically let your clients know (in person, by phone, or in writing) the tasks you have done to insure their project's success.

One consultant adds a detailed list of work completed to the bottom of his invoices with the wording, "Professional services include: . . . ." This list serves as an acknowledgment of his work and provides an additional perceived value to the client.

Some examples include the following:

- Research preparation
- Telephone and conference calls
- Travel time
- Design work
- Routine reports
- Surveys, interviews, and questionnaires
- Organization of files and records
- Reading material
- Material development
- Review of company records
- Internal stragegy meetings
- Investigating the competition

6. Be Seen as a Researcher in Your Field

Being identified as a researcher and one who contributes to the education and advancement of your field of interest will greatly increase referrals. Devote time and effort to designing and implementing research projects that provide valuable information to those who read and those who publish your information.

Such research need not be highly sophisticated or time consuming. Simple opinion surveys or questionnaires that measure trend information or point out directions in thinking or behavior are often sufficient. They help you create recognition for you as a knowledgeable resource at the cutting edge of your area of expertise.

7. Make Yourself Known to Influential Sources

Increase referrals by becoming known to influential sources whom you have not yet had the opportunity to meet. If they are sufficiently prestigious and influential, your association with them will create a halo or association relationship that will benefit you. Even more important is the fact that you may have the opportunity to work with them directly or benefit from the referrals sent your way.

A proven, effective way to make contact and to influence those you do not know, especially influential people, is to request their participation in your research or writing project. Plan a specific project and contact the influential experts for an interview. If you attribute the experts' thinking, data, or remarks in a document that is to be published, be sure to set up another meeting to review the information you have used.

At your first meeting, do not solicit business or referrals. Instead, use the initial contact as a basis for developing a professional relationship. In the future, you can meet again for similar purposes. Meanwhile, add their names to your circulation lists.

In the first or subsequent meetings, you will inevitably have an opportunity to describe your work and services. This opportunity can then lead to direct business or referrals.

8. Turn Wasted Time to Productive Marketing

Turn wasted television or air travel time into productive marketing. Photocopy an item of interest to prospective clients and use this time to write them a personal note and mail it to them. Hand write (don't word process) your note and envelope. Use a stamp, not a meter, for maximum benefit. This personal touch results in their thinking about you, even being indebted to you, and it produces direct business or referrals.

Look at every item that comes across your desk as being of potential interest to clients, prospects, and referral sources. Ask yourself, "How does this information impact those that I provide services to?" Interpret the impact of them in your handwritten note, and mail it. Keep thinking about your clients and you will cause them to keep thinking about you.

9. Work Your Rolodex®

Divide your personal telephone directory or Rolodex® into twelve sections—about two alphabetical letters a month. Set aside two or three hours each month to call each person on the list (January is A and B, February is C and D, and so forth) who may be a source of business or referrals. These should be people to whom you have not spoken in the last 90 to 120 days.

What's the purpose? Just to say hello and to inquire about their well being. Do *not* attempt to solicit business. If circumstances permit, casually mention an interesting project or beneficial referral received. The conversation should end without their feeling that they have been marketed.

This is an excellent way of staying in touch, in a professional way, with people in a position to benefit you. Some will initially communicate caution, awaiting your sales pitch. When it becomes obvious that you are not pitching, they will relax and open up.

Avoid the temptation to look at every business card received or every contact as a source for referrals. As in all areas of marketing, be selective. There is only so much time available for marketing and business development. Use your time wisely by being selective. On the other hand, do not be too quick to dismiss potential sources of future business without giving them an opportunity to show ways in which they might help you.

As your expertise increases in getting good referrals and as the numbers grow, you may find it effective to divide your personal sources into several categories. You may decide to set up lists according to their degree of importance. Consider communicating with them with regard to their degree of importance. That is, the more important the source becomes, the more frequent the contact. Of course, these sources can be moved to different lists based on the circumstances and experience you have with them.

10. Enclose Two Business Cards in All Your Correspondence

Of all the marketing aids available today, your business card remains the least expensive selling tool you can use. In fact, you should enclose not one, but two cards in *everything* that goes outbound from your office. Here's why:

Often prospects and clients need one business card for their card file, Rolodex, or card file book. The second card is often used more creatively. It may be kept handy in a Day Timer or on the credenza. And once in a while the second card is sent to a co-worker, prospect, or friend—along with a recommendation for looking into your services. If one card in a thousand generates more business, it's a win.

Keep sending two cards—even to existing clients. Keeping your phone ringing means keeping "top of mind awareness." Where else can you do it for just the pennies invested in two business cards?

11. Help Clients Get in Touch with You

Despite your efforts to communicate pertinent information about the precise nature of the services you provide, your telephone number and address, etc., referral sources often don't remember or have access to that information when making a referral. Take the necessary steps that make it easy to obtain this information. List your name and company in directories and other resources so that referral sources can look up the necessary information and encounter it *quickly* and *easily*.

Be sure to list your name and company in the yellow pages of the major telephone directory in your market area. An expensive, large and flashy ad isn't necessary and could be counterproductive. But a listing or small ad spelling out the services that you provide should, if properly written, produce a number of potential leads.

Be listed in *all* trade and professional directories that reach your target market and that you can get into for little or no charge. Many who need your services don't know how to find someone with your expertise. Facilitate connections by listing in directories. More than half of all professional directories will allow you to be listed free of charge—it's a service to members.

12. Provide "Request for Information" Cards to Advertise Your Services

Not everyone you encounter will have a business card. And you will meet some who have already given away their in-pocket supply. Avoid their embarrassments by carrying "request for information" cards. These could be postal cards with your address and phone number on one side. The reverse side should provide a place for the user's name, title, firm, address, phone number, and other information. When someone desires the technical or professional information that you could provide (or agreed to make available), simply say something like, "Please fill out this card and I will see that this information is mailed to you first thing tomorrow."

13. Include Your Phone Number on *Everything* You Distribute

A caller announced that he heard a consultant speak some seven years ago. Not only had he been favorably impressed, but he had saved the seminar workbook containing the consultant's phone number for all those years. What if the caller hadn't had a handout bearing the consultant's name and phone number?

The lesson learned? First, make sure that *everything* you make, print, mail, or distribute contains at least your name and phone number.

In addition to printing your name, address, and phone number on everything, invest in a roll of pressure-sensitive labels to affix to those miscellaneous items, mailouts, giveaways, article reprints, freebie books, audio tapes, and gifts of all kinds.

The day your name and phone number are everywhere is the day you can be sure your calendar will be full . . . maybe they will even generate a lead seven years from now.

14. Ask Contacts to Recommend You Directly to Prospects

It is far better to be called than to call. When people suggest that you contact someone because your services would be of benefit, urge the individuals to make the initial contact. Suggest to the referring sources that they take the responsibility of communicating on your behalf.

But make it easy for them. Consider drafting a letter that they can give to prospective clients. A cover letter to the referral sources may say that the prospect letter communicates preliminary information about your services. And state that you are providing the prospect letter to the referring sources as a matter of convenience.

You will encourage more and better referrals if you can convince the referring sources to believe that they will benefit more from the connection than you. That is, you communicate an attitude that, while you are pleased to have referrals, your financial and professional well being are not dependent on this or any other referral.

15. Be Subtle If You Cold Call

Cold calling to get an appointment with a prospective client is often unproductive. Few have time to talk with "sales people." Cold calls also give the impression that you need the business.

Instead, call and arrange an appointment to interview the prospect in connection with an article you are writing for a magazine, for your newsletter, or for a research project. Make sure the interviewee receives copies of the finished work.

Business is usually given to people whom one has met professionally. During your interview, you might discreetly steer the conversation to what you do and how the prospect may someday have a need for your services.

16. Make the First Client Meeting Productive

Make sure clients realize your time is as valuable or even more valuable than theirs. People have greater respect for and are willing to do business with those they regard as busy and important. One way to get clients to view you in this light is to ensure that *you* interview *them* before they interview you. Controlling the first meeting is one way to increase the probability of getting the business.

When first meeting prospective clients, be sure to communicate whether or not there is a charge for the initial meeting. If you do charge, make sure they understand the amount and payment terms.

In the first meeting with prospective clients, focus on what they need to make their problems disappear and how to take advantage of the challenges they are facing. Don't waste your prospects' time by providing a verbal résumé. If they need information about your skills and experience, they will certainly ask.

17. Match Your Services (and Your Appearance) to Your Prospective Client's

Do your homework. Make sure that you obtain prior information about your prospect before your first meeting. Contact individuals who have done business with the prospect's company. Their information assists you in evaluating the needs of the prospective client. Your clients will be impressed that you were interested enough to take the time to get background information on them. The quality of your marketing materials should equal the type of materials that your prospect would use when marketing.

Dress the way your client or prospect dresses (within reason). Don't be overly formal or informal. If you don't know, it is better to err on the side of being more formal than informal. This formality gives you the impression of being a professional.

Also if you are unsure of the type of dress, arrive outside the prospects' offices a day or two before your scheduled meeting. Observe the appearance of the staff, their punctuality, and the look of the office. This assessment gives you an opportunity to observe the company prior to your arrival.

18. Make a *Great* First Impression

As the saying goes, "you never get a second chance to make a good first impression." If that statement is true—and it is—why don't more businesses practice it? Just try a few random phone calls to businesses and observe the first impression they make on the phone. Horrible!

Here is a proven system to make certain you always make a good impression on the phone:

First, don't ever, ever, *ever* let anyone answer your phone who isn't trained and committed to being the best.

Then . . .

- Hesitate. Clear your mind. Answer on the third ring ready to sell.
- Answer with a smile. Your smile will convey your enthusiasm.
- Give a greeting, your company name, and your name. Example: "Good Morning, ABC Company, Jack Smith speaking."
- Be patient with callers. Remember they called you because you're the *pro*! Be patient when answering questions . . . your attitude is showing!
- Close the sale! Capture the customer's name and phone number and agree on follow-up action. Making a *great* first impression is *critical* to making the sale.

Bonus tip: When training new staff, outline these points and post them above their phones. Each time the phone rings, they'll be reminded to use the points until they become habit.

19. Remember that Your Best Prospects are Your Current Clients

Devote a minimum of 30 minutes a week (uncompensated) for each client. Show additional ways you can benefit every client through a mini-proposal (letter or memo). By doing this, you are reminding your clients how *valuable* you are and that there are *other* services available that you can provide.

When you next meet, take a few minutes to discuss your mini-proposal. Test for interest. It may lead to additional business right away or in the near future. You won't always get an immediate response. However, after several weeks of receiving your mini-proposals, your impact will be greater.

20. Peg Your Fees In the Client's Mind

New clients and those not familiar with professional fee schedules often gasp when they learn how much speakers, consultants, and professional service providers must charge for their work. Use a positioning technique to help prospects or clients think of you on a higher level.

Here is an example of this technique:

> "Mr. Prospect, in answer to how much I charge for this work, be aware that my fees are affordable—similar to what you would probably pay your CPA or attorney."

Then go on to build features and benefits of the work you plan to do. Close by reminding your prospects or clients that your work will pay big dividends and therefore isn't an expense—they must think of it as an *investment*.

Bonus tip: When appropriate, close with a written recap of all the benefits your prospects can expect to receive from their investment.

21. Sell Skeptics by Guaranteeing their Satisfaction

After a long telephone conversation, it was clear that a prospect was still skeptical. While a friend had highly recommended the consultant to address a group's annual conference in Winnipeg, the prospect had not seen, met, or heard the consultant speak. While many of his questions had been answered during the call, the prospect still had doubts. Add to that the risk of paying a substantial speaker's fee and travel costs. If the consultant bombed, the prospect would lose all around. To salvage such a situation required a bold move. What was it? The consultant told him, "You only pay if I deliver."

Offer prospects and clients this bold guarantee and blow their skepticism away. In the case of this prospect, the consultant agreed that performance and pay would be based on a survey from the audience. If the consultant met the promised goals, the check would be in the mail. And if the consultant failed, there would be a long trip home with an empty wallet.

When constructing bold guarantees, be careful of these things:

1. Make certain you have some way to *specifically measure* the performance you are targeting. In the above case, the audience rated the consultant's program on a one to ten scale. An audience average of seven or more was the target.
2. Be sure you can *influence* or even *control* the outcome. Because consultants don't normally implement their recommendations, someone else could sabotage even the best of plans.
3. Be careful of people who will only use and *abuse* you. It is sad that consultants need to be constantly alert to someone trying to deceive and cheat them. Fortunately those people are a minority.

Bonus tip: For super-skeptical prospects, consider adding a delayed payment clause to their agreement—"You pay me no money until you have proven results in hand."

22. Respond Promptly to All Correspondence and Phone Calls

Respond to all correspondence received (from clients, prospects and others) as promptly as possible, and certainly *within seven days.* Same-day or next-morning response is even better.

This prompt response enhances your image even more. You will be seen as one who handles all aspects of his business relationships with speed and reliability. If you need more time to give a full answer in your correspondence, at least acknowledge receipt of the letter and communicate the date that you will be able to provide a substantive response.

Answer all telephone calls received (again, from clients, prospects, and others) quickly. If possible, return the call on the day received or certainly by the next day.

Responding to requests for information within 24 hours can result in a substantial increase in the number of signed clients. Prospects do not usually plan ahead. When they contact you, they want *action* . . . and they want that action *now.*

23. Make Prospects Think You Don't Need the Work

Communicate an air of indifference to prospective clients regarding whether you get their business. This attitude is difficult when you really are not indifferent, but you will be more desirable to prospects when it appears (to them) that they need you more than you need them. The most successful consultants are indifferent.

The best way to be truly indifferent is to have viable options for how you will spend your time. Devote time each week to developing one or more proprietary products or services (such as seminars, newsletters, manuals, software, etc.) that you can sell. These products and services not only give you viable options but they will help you to determine the true value of your time and allow you to set the most appropriate fee to charge your clients.

24. Learn to Accept Praise and to Say Thank You

Develop the art of accepting thanks and praise gracefully. When complimented, learn to express a simple thanks for the favorable words. It is not appropriate to explain why, in your estimation, thanks are not really due. Acknowledge your appreciation for the kind remarks made. Express your gratitude in being able to assist the individual giving the praise.

By failing to accept thanks when given, you give the impression to the person giving the praise and to those listening that you are undeserving of it. You inadvertently raise questions about your ability if you feel you are unworthy. Those who give the unacknowledged praise will be less inclined to do you a favor if they feel their praise is unappreciated. And they will certainly be less inclined to refer business your way.

25. Close the Sale Definitively

Many professionals fail to inform the prospective client of the desired response. In other words, *they fail to close the sale.* Make sure you communicate what *action* you want the prospect to take. While selling your services by letter, in a phone call, or in person, don't forget to spell out exactly what action you want the prospect to take next.

Even the most sophisticated prospects need to be guided. Make it easier for them by directing them to ask for your services.

Bonus tip: Memorize this rule: "People want to be told what to do, and will do what they are told."

Chapter 2

Marketing Don'ts

26. Avoid Overcommitting Yourself

Avoid the "walk on water" syndrome. Professionals who have been successful in handling a problem for a client are sometimes thought to walk on water, to be invincible. As a result, they receive requests to provide services that are really outside their field of expertise—even when they protest their suitability for such additional responsibilities. Nonetheless, they often agree to provide the requested additional service.

Flattery is sometimes a difficult environment in which to make the most appropriate decisions. Such additional services, for obvious reasons, are often perceived by the client as being less effective than the original service provided. Avoid going beyond the boundaries of your expertise—regardless of your client's urging.

27. Know Your Limitations

Avoid any professional assignment if you are not *fully technically competent* or if you lack all resources necessary for producing the desired accomplishment. Your image is *vital* for future business and referrals. Do not let your immediate need for income influence your decision to work for clients with whom you have personality conflicts, clients whose staff has conflicts with yours or clients who are not likely to be satisfied.

Increase your credibility by recommending that your services not be used for certain needs your prospects may have. When clients can accomplish things on their own or if other professionals can provide certain services more efficiently than you, *let the prospects know*. They will have more respect for you in the long run. Know your limitations.

28. Admit When You Are Wrong

Be willing to admit mistakes and errors. Bring any bad news to the attention of your client *promptly* and *professionally*. You are only human, and it is inevitable that from time to time you will make errors or be in a position of bearing bad news. Handling these difficulties in a professional fashion increases your image and stimulates referrals, particularly with more sophisticated clients.

29. Watch Your Ego

Prospective referral sources do not appreciate seeing you solicit referrals. Avoid describing your talents and capabilities directly, as though you were delivering a commercial. Instead, concentrate your communications with a discussion of how you have produced *benefits* and how you've been involved in *working with others* where excellent results have been obtained. Resist the tendency to take full credit or to be egocentric. It will be obvious that your role was instrumental. Being indirect is usually best.

Referrals are rarely made to those with too big an ego. In working with clients, avoid always being in the limelight. Allow clients and their staff to take credit and to receive recognition for some accomplishments produced. Those in a position to refer business and engage your services for future projects will know of your involvement and contributions, and you will be seen as easier to work with. Throughout your involvement, and certainly at the end of a given project, you will find subtle and professional ways to remind clients of your importance relative to the accomplishments.

30. Don't Make Your Business Card an Advertising Billboard

Avoid using your business card as an advertising billboard. Don't list the 29 different services that you provide to your clients. The list would make you look like a jack-of-all-trades. The less said the better. Descriptions of services provided have a tendency to reduce the number of people who will have an interest in contacting you.

Sometimes the best business card says very little. It makes the recipient curious about what you do. This curiosity leads to questions, and questions provide you with an opportunity to relate your services to the needs and interests of each prospect.

31. Never, *Never* Use a Résumé

Never use a résumé to promote your services. You may have to develop a résumé to satisfy the files of an existing client, but it is a disastrous first marketing piece.

Résumés often wind up in the hands of the wrong people—the personnel or human resources department. Unless you are interested in providing your services to personnel/HRD, having them make the decision about further contact with you is usually a disaster.

Résumés often generate form response letters—"not now, maybe later, we will keep you in our files." There are not enough file cabinets to permit all those who claim to keep you on file to really do so. And, even if there were, they couldn't find your résumé when needed.

As a professional, you should use brochures or capability statements. Doing so will increase the response to your efforts enormously.

32. Don't Promote Yourself to the Personnel Department

Do not promote your services to the personnel department (unless you are an advisor or consultant to personnel departments). *Always* promote your services to the executive or manager responsible for seeing that the desired result is accomplished.

The personnel or human resources department, like all corporate departments, has its own agenda. Building a large, full-time staff is important to justify continued funding growth for personnel. Independent professionals get in the way of that objective. Moreover, personnel is a support function. Always go right to the manager or executive responsible for getting the work done.

33. Don't Use Lunch Invitations to Sell Your Services

Avoid inviting prospects to lunch to sell your services. They really don't want to be put in a position which makes them think they are likely to be sold. Instead, invite them to be your guest for lunch to advise *you* on some issue about which they are knowledgeable. The conversation will inevitably turn to what you do and how it relates to their needs.

Most valuable professional relationships develop because of *mutual respect* between the parties. You can be effective in general, and certainly in marketing, by being an advice *taker* as well as an advice *giver*.

34. Don't Be Too Rational in Your Sales Pitch

If you are having trouble convincing prospects about the wisdom of your ideas and making use of your services, your marketing may be too rational. We sometimes think selling professional services to the business market is a totally rational sell. It isn't always. Your marketing may have to appeal to the "nonrational" needs of the prospect, with particular attention on how making use of your services will benefit the prospect *personally*.

Emotion and personal benefits are major factors in securing sales in all markets—not just the consumer market. It is your responsibility to explain, with subtlety, how your services will benefit the client organization and the decision maker responsible for seeing to it that you get the business.

35. Don't Use the Same Solution to Every Problem

When working with prospects, make sure they understand you will customize your services just for them. They don't want a "canned soup" approach. All prospects believe that their situations are unique and worthy of special, custom responses and solutions. Even though you have handled the same problems hundreds of times, you must be a "professional" Broadway actor giving the 500th performance as though it were opening night.

When talking with prospects, avoid the trap of routine answers to common questions. You give the appearance of lumping the prospects' problems into categories, which shows a general lack of interest. Don't waste their time. If you don't have anything uniquely interesting and creative to say or ask, then you probably shouldn't be talking to the prospects in the first place.

36. Don't Get Stale: Keep Up to Date In Your Field

Work on *staying fresh*, different, and perceptive. Spend a half day, at least twice a year, walking around the reference room of a major university library. Pull interesting books, directories, and guides off the shelf and examine them. Most major libraries today have audio tape sections: make the most of your travel time in the car by listening to other professionals in your field. By constantly working on new ideas through books or tapes, you will find a host of interesting marketing opportunities and new services that you can provide to your clients.

37. Never Assume Anything When Communicating with Clients

Nothing is more stressful or potentially disastrous than misunderstandings with a prospect or client. The majority of such problems come from communication gaps. Here is a rule that can start you toward closing those critical gaps:

"The greatest problem with communication is to assume that it took place."

Boost your professional image and bulletproof your client relationships by becoming a "communication nut." Follow up conversations with a simple memo, note, or letter. And anytime you even *suspect* a communication misunderstanding, move at lightning speed to clear the air. Invest in forms, stationery, and every tool available to be understood. And stay on the cutting edge with communication technology from sky pagers to fax mail, from voice mail to cellular phones.

Remember the rule . . . and master a key word—*invest*. You are *investing* in communication which can *make* or *break* your professional practice.

38. Avoid Being a Lap Dog to Clients

Do not be a lap dog consultant or advisor. Those professionals who are too flexible, too available, too bending, rarely get the business. Do business on your own terms and stick to your guns. But make sure that your business practices are reasonable and in line with what the competition is offering.

If you are perceived as too cooperative and too flexible, prospects and clients won't respect you or your independence. Don't allow yourself to be perceived as a hard-to-work-with-prima-donna, but be sure to communicate the independence and standards that make you desirable.

39. Don't Appear Hungry for Business

Don't beg for business! No one wants to do business with someone who appears to be needy or hungry. When setting a meeting time with clients or prospects, don't open your calendar and say, "Anytime next week would be fine." You give the impression that you have nothing to do. Instead, say, "I am free to meet with you on Tuesday from 1:00 until 3:00 or Friday between 9:00 and 11:00. Which would be best for you?"

When selling your services, don't talk too much. You should be speaking 40% of the time or less.

Talk about past *successes*, not about previous clients. Don't tell prospects about the insider information of clients you have worked for in the past. They will assume that if you are talking about past clients now, *they* will be the subject of discussion in the future.

Hint: Record a few of your presentations and listen later to make sure you don't spend too much time talking and too little time listening.

40. *Never* Badmouth Your Competition

Never make any disparaging remarks about the competition or past clients. Remember, if you do not have anything nice to say, say nothing. Derogatory remarks suggest unprofessional behavior and will hurt referrals . . . and eventually your business reputation. There are always other means of communicating caution to others—by saying little or nothing, or by the creative use of intonation.

When Oprah Winfrey asked the founder of Weight Watchers® why her diet plan was better than all the others, she had a perfect national forum to put down her competition. Instead, she eloquently commented, "I don't know all the others well enough to evaluate them; however, let me tell you why I believe the Weight Watchers program has helped millions of people meet their goals." She then explained at length the strengths and benefits of Weight Watchers proven programs.

Upon joining the Eagles, a fraternal organization, members are sworn to this pledge:

"If I can not speak well of an Eagle, I will not speak ill of him."

Accept that challenge today when discussing competition:

"If I can't say something good about my competitors, I will say nothing."

It is all too easy to criticize. You don't make yourself taller by cutting down your competition.

CHAPTER 3

Doing Direct Mail

41. Develop a "Most Wanted" List of Prospects

With thousands of rapists, muggers and killers on the loose in our country, why does the FBI still have their 10 most wanted list? The short answer—to *focus*.

Ever go out to look for 5,000 different bad guys? At best, you might catch only a few. For the same reason, you do need to be marketing to a large universe, but for *quantum-leap results*, try focusing on your own "most wanted" list.

You can have 5, 10, 25, or 50 on your short list; just make sure it is a small enough list so that you can hunt down prospects *daily*.

Some consultants target their Top 50 prospects. This select group gets very regular mailings, extra bulletins, phone calls, and special items such as free products and books.

Bonus tip: Often clients like to know they are on your select hit list. If appropriate, tell them that you consider them "extra special."

42. Develop Promotional Brochures to Meet Specific Needs

Write a separate brochure for each market area you serve. Concentrate on the *benefits* you can provide to that *specific* type of client you are targeting. General brochures too often are not specific or relevant to motivate a desired answer.

Everyone would like to do something once and be done with it. Effective marketing, however, requires that you *target* your audience. The more specific your promotion to the interest of the prospect, the greater the reaction. Target marketing will significantly increase your promotional response. Targeting an audience takes more time and effort, but it really pays!

43. Encourage Prospects to Respond Immediately

In advertising and direct mail campaigns, include a direct response form, which can increase your return. The easier you make it for the prospect to request more information, the greater your response.

When promoting your services, include an ***"act now!"*** kicker to increase attention. Interested prospects (like everyone else) tend to procrastinate. Give them an extra benefit by acting *now* rather than later, when they are more likely to forget to call.

44. Don't Conduct Mass Mailings

Be careful about mass mailings to cold leads. They are rarely successful. If you must try this method, then test your promotions in *very* small quantities. If it works, continue. If not, research into the successful marketing techniques of the professionals and implement them.

Avoid falling prey to those who will provide you with a "proven" mailing system of 10,000 hot prospects for your services. While direct mail marketing can be very effective for the sale of products, it rarely works for professional services. When you target your marketing efforts to a select few, who have successfully used and appreciated your services, you will receive better results.

Some consultants have developed a list of their Top 50 clients to whom they target their mailings with outstanding results! But they don't just stop at one mailing. They continue to mail on a regular monthly basis, constantly providing new material to review. By limiting their marketing audience to the "tried and true," they accomplish the following:

- Clients are continually reminded of the consultants' availability to meet *individual* needs.
- Clients know they are *valued* members of a very *selective* list.
- Clients constantly receive *updates* on new material and research findings.

Remember: The more *specifically* you target your market, the better the results you will achieve.

45. Increase the Impact of Your Sales Letters

When writing marketing letters, increase the impact with a handwritten postscript (P.S.). It will result in your letter *instantly* grabbing the reader's attention and possibly being read first.

When preparing a sales letter, consider using a P.S. that does not clearly communicate but forces the reader to go back and read the entire letter. For example:

"P.S. Johnson accomplished this in 1976."

Whether through the P.S. or by other means, you have just a moment to attract the reader's attention. *Be creative.* Test different ideas. Learning to write an intriguing P.S. will enhance the effectiveness of your marketing significantly.

46. Write Detailed, Yet Creative, Sales Letters

In sales letters, multiple-page letters usually outperform single-page letters. Don't be afraid to use a lot of copy in your sales letters. Some people are fearful about doing so. They are concerned that the reader won't read the entire letter. Research clearly demonstrates, however, that an interested prospect will read a great deal and that extra copy *increases* response.

To write an effective sales letter, consider these points:

1. *Be creative.* Consider including an item of curiosity and creativity. For example, onc consultant sent chattering teeth to attract the attention of her clients and show the importance of customers' comments. The teeth created tremendous results in promoting a series of Word-of-Mouth marketing seminars.
2. *Include postscripts.* The P.S. helps raise questions and gets clients to call. For example, one P.S. referred to an "Uncle Luigi Story." Many clients called inquiring about the story's contents.
3. *Grab the readers' attention.* The beginning information is the most valuable. It must interest readers so they will read further.
4. *Don't worry that your letter is too long.* Length does not affect readership. Some people hesitate to use more then one page. If it is necessary to get your information on several pages, then by all means, do it. Well-written letters will encourage readership regardless of length.
5. *Make sure names and titles are spelled correctly.* No one is interested in a letter that contains an incorrect inside address.

47. Consider Starting a Newsletter

Write and publish a monthly, bimonthly, or quarterly newsletter. The newsletter is an excellent device to maintain regular contact with all potential referral sources as well as those in a position to use your services directly.

The newsletter need not be expensive or difficult to produce. Some of the most effective letters used by your peers are nothing more than provocative, philosophical thoughts, word processed or typed on standard letterhead, and just one to four pages in length. A more sophisticated format or different length may be useful too.

Place those you wish to influence and to contact regularly on your circulation list. To be effective, your newsletter must be good and interesting. It should not be perceived as direct advertising, but the *indirect* promotional benefit is obvious.

48. Keep Contacts in Your Communication Loop

Keep contacts who have referred clients in your communication loop. Obviously, it would not be appropriate to communicate details or confidences related to the services that you have provided. But an occasional follow-up telephone call or written communication that informs the referring source about how beneficial the referral has become will stimulate future referrals. Besides, the acknowledgement is simply common courtesy.

Keep prospects, former clients, and others familiar with your successes. Find a way to communicate awards, honors, presentations, new contracts, research results, and breakthroughs. Your successes make you seem more valuable and people will be more likely to do business with you in the future. One way of communicating this information, which is unobtrusive and which does not seem boastful, is to put helpful individuals on the circulation list to receive your monthly, bimonthly, or quarterly newsletter.

Chapter 4

Networking

49. Network Productively

Networking is good for business, but don't spend too much time networking—and especially avoid spending time on unproductive networking. Standing around with a cocktail glass is not productive. Position yourself to be the *leader* of the network, not the follower. If you desire to serve small clients or impoverished clients profitably, then think about setting up a group of clients with similar needs, and provide your services on a group basis that all can afford.

No one says that you must join someone's network. Think about starting your own, and hand-pick members for your business advantage.

Consider scheduling a series of meetings (perhaps four to six a year) and invite good clients and prospects to attend without charge. Give each meeting a theme, such as "How to Increase Your Collections with the Telephone" or "Thriving in the 1990s." Bring these people together under your leadership to discuss the issue of concern. The discussion will give you a change to show your stuff and help identify the consulting needs of the participants.

50. Join Associations, but Be Selective

Join one or two professional or trade associations comprised of your prospective clients and referral sources. Do so *only* if you are willing to become *active, noticed,* and *powerful* in the association. Work your way up the power structure and contribute generously to be noticed and seen as a resource. Avoid wasting valuable time as an unnoticed member of many organizations.

Don't waste time and effort joining dozens of organizations just to say you are a member. Concentrate networking efforts to maximum advantage and productivity.

51. Develop Positive Relationships with Movers and Shakers

Scan newspapers, magazines, and newsletters in your market area. Identify the names of people who have made significant contributions to your field of specialty. Form some communication with them to gain further information about their work. These contacts help you to develop relationships with the movers and shakers. They also assist you in being known and recognized, and they lead to desirable referrals.

Do not wait for others to take the initiative. Professionals and authorities always want to discuss their work with interested individuals. In most cases, these experts will be receptive and open to developing a relationship with you—as long as they perceive your interest to be legitimate. Make the call *now*—and offer to buy lunch.

52. After You Meet, Follow Up

After meeting people at a social or business situation, *promptly* send a personal note expressing your pleasure in meeting them. These notes communicate that your meeting was significant enough for you to remember some aspect of your conversation with them.

Do not give the appearance of a form letter stating, "nice to have met you." Speak to the individuals *personally* and *specifically* about your areas of interest in the conversations you had with them.

Unless requested, the communications should *not* appear as direct solicitations to provide you with business or professional advantage. The best and most meaningful referrals come from having *already* established a professional relationship. Don't jump on the potential opportunity too fast. You could hurt your future opportunities.

53. Make Yourself Visible at Conferences

When attending conferences, seminars, and similar events where you will have the opportunity to be seen and heard, turn such opportunities into widespread professional exposure. Help yourself to a little piece of the stage. Position yourself in the meeting room at a location where you will be noticed and easily heard and seen. The front left-hand corner is one very desirable spot.

Manage to stand, speak out and make comments that are provocative, noteworthy, and sometimes controversial. The *quality* of what you say is much more important than the quantity. Don't turn another's seminar into your own, but a few well placed, "surely to be talked about" remarks will be beneficial.

When the session breaks for coffee, lunch, or at the end of the day, make yourself *accessible* and *visible*. Encourage those who were present to engage in conversation.

54. Review Your Past to Find Prospects and Referral Sources

Mine potential clients and referral sources out of your more distant past. Surely you know people with whom you have not communicated in years who might make good referral sources. Just because you have not communicated of late does not mean that you should not start now.

Make a list of at least two or three people from each of the following groups:

- Neighborhood friends from childhood
- Classmates (elementary, junior high, high school, and college)
- Past teachers and professors
- Former employers, co-workers, subordinates
- Past business contacts—vendors, competitors, and financial contacts
- Past contacts from charitable, social service, and purely social relationships
- Previous customers and prospects
- Others from your past who are now in positions of (potential) authority, power, and influence.

Select one or more means to renew contact with these people and implement the selected strategies. You may be reluctant to re-initiate contact because of feelings about your past relationship. But old fears, failure to be in the right clique, etc., have long been forgotten and the contacts will be pleased that you made the effort to reestablish the relationship.

55. Think Twice Before Mixing Business and Social Relationships

Exercise restraint in turning clients into social friends. The close working relationship and shared interests often encourage doing so, but it can hurt the professionalism with which services are delivered, and it can have a negative impact upon their willingness to refer business. Conversely, many find it desirable to establish a firm policy of not doing business with friends.

Many professionals are able to develop excellent referrals and direct business from their social contacts. If you are comfortable in doing so, you should probably take advantage of the opportunity. Some can turn an afternoon on the golf course or a lunch at the city/country club into excellent future business.

If you have difficulty doing so or feel uncomfortable in such situations, there are many other ways to develop referrals. Don't try to develop referrals with activities that you find uncomfortable. Your lack of comfort will be obvious and your success will be limited accordingly. Devote effort employing referral marketing strategies where you are both relaxed *and* effective.

CHAPTER 5

Cultivating Referrals

56. Spread the Word to Advertise Your Services

Cultivate referrals through broadcast power. People of influence and authority—such as association executives, editors, and conference chairs—can magnify your referral opportunities significantly. A good referral marketing program should devote most of its effort to influencing these sources. Such individuals can provide help in publicizing your abilities and professionalism. These endorsements will build confidence in the minds of those who are uncertain about their ability to evaluate your worth.

Encourage multiple referrals. Hearing that you are an expert in your field from just one source may be encouraging to a prospective client. Hearing the same message from several sources is convincing. Whenever possible, orchestrate multiple recommendations of your abilities to a targeted prospect.

57. Obtain Referrals Before You Need Them

Don't postpone developing a referral marketing system because you are too busy or too successful. Time and energy spent on developing a strong base will pay off handsomely. The best results will accrue over time. And the best time to build a solid foundation of referral business is not when you *need* the business, but when you *don't* need the business.

An important motivation for developing a strong referral marketing system is not just to acquire *new* clients, but to develop *more interesting* and *select* clients who provide challenging assignments. Even those professionals who have more business than they can handle have found it beneficial to work on referral marketing. Experience has taught them that having the right clientele has strong economic and professional advantages.

Work on making referral marketing easy and creative. Many who know the benefits of a good referral markcting system do not develop one because they lack the internal systems or procedures that help to implement strategies in an effective, easy, and cost-efficient manner. Technology can make this happen. Develop or obtain the system necessary for your practice. It could be the most important investment you make in business development.

58. Ask Current Clients to Refer Potential New Clients

Current clients are an excellent, but often forgotten, source of referral business and follow-up or add-on business. Your regular and ongoing interaction with clients and their confidence in your abilities make them a resource for referral business that is often unequalled.

Special attention should be devoted to mining this pool of potential business. Set aside time each week for marketing activities that will cause this special resource to be motivated to refer business your way or to engage your services for additional work. Here, as elsewhere, avoid actions that would convey the suggestion that you are in need of the business. Be creative in suggesting and exploring new ideas, concepts, and approaches that would be of significant benefit to your clients or those with whom your clients interact (internally and externally).

59. Consider Prospects as Referral Sources—and Vice Versa

You may view someone as a referral source who might also be a prospect for your services *directly*. And someone whom you have categorized as a prospect may never use your services but may be a bountiful source of referrals. Don't be quick to categorize *anyone*. Some of your prospects may be unwilling to make use of your services until after they have referred you to another source. After they have obtained an evaluation of your services from that source, then they may be willing to work with you.

60. Promote Your Competition

Expend energy promoting your competition for referrals, subcontracts or joint assignments. In many fields a portion of all new business can come from the competition. Recognize that competitors' marketing efforts may result in:

- assignments that they view as being *outside* their field of specialty
- business they are *too busy* to handle
- projects of such scope that they need to retain the services of another professional *to work jointly.*

When involved in a subcontract or joint assignment with another professional, avoid activities that appear as attempts to market yourself for future business. If clients perceive that working with you at a later date is more desirable, they will contact you. But marketing to competitors' clients directly is inappropriate and will hurt future business that may come from your peers. This inappropriate behavior will also diminish your professionalism in the eyes of the clients you are both serving.

When you hire subcontractors, make sure you have a written agreement that includes a noncompete clause. This clause protects you from their setting up shop on their own and taking *your* clients with them.

61. Always Maintain Good Relationships with Your Referral Sources

The rewards of a good referral marketing system are great. In time you will be in a position where most of your new business comes from referrals. Private practice has its ups and downs, however, so don't permit yourself to become complacent. Renew your good fortune by continuing to employ the strategies that have made you successful.

As you obtain a larger and better quality base of clients as a result of your marketing efforts, remember to show the same standards of professionalism, good taste, courtesy, and humility that produced the benefits you are now enjoying.

Avoid suggesting that you have become so important and successful that you can afford to be arrogant and impolite. Remember the saying: "Be nice to people on the way up, because you will meet the very same people on your way down."

62. Respond to Clients Promptly and Politely

Encourage referrals by establishing a reputation for being prompt, paying attention to details, and practicing proper business etiquette. Answer all correspondence within a day or two, return all phone calls within one or two days, and send thank-you notes when appropriate. Make sure you send these *promptly*. Follow up on all requests for information that you promised to provide.

Be recognized for your ability to respond to others in a timely fashion. Doing so is the sign of a true professional. You will develop respect in your industry that motivates others to speak highly of you. And that will help keep your phone ringing.

63. Develop Referral Sources by Asking for Advice

Develop your referral sources by turning the tables. Don't call or write potential sources to set up an appointment with the intention of asking them to refer business your way. These valuable sources will avoid you like the plague. Instead, set up an appointment to solicit their advice and counsel on an issue of relevance to your practice or intellectual and professional development.

People are flattered when asked to influence your thinking. In the course of your meeting, you will get around to explaining what you do and how you obtain business. You can plant the most subtle suggestions about your receptivity to their referrals (or direct business) and harvest the benefits later.

64. Do Not Become a Jack-of-all-Trades

Your referral sources consider you to be highly professional and an expert in your specific field. They recommend you to others on that basis. Therefore, you should avoid giving the impression that you are a jack-of-all-trades, willing to do anything asked—whether or not it is in your area of specialty.

When describing your services to referral sources, or to clients directly, communicate that there are certain services you are unwilling to provide. Although you may convey the impression that there a number of things that you can do, it may not always be cost effective for clients to make use of your services. Also indicate that there are services that you are capable of showing clients how to do internally, thus allowing them to avoid expensive, outside services. This offer displays your concern for achieving what you perceive to be in the best interests of your clients.

65. Let Contacts Know You Desire Referrals

Find a professional and comfortable way to let your clients know that you appreciate referrals. Also show your clients how to make referrals. When improperly handled, referrals are worthless. When done with professional finesse, however, they are *invaluable.*

One of the major reasons professionals do not receive referrals—even though clients find their services of great benefit—is that they have not shown their clients the proper way to make a referral. When clients do not know how or fail to recognize their importance to you, they cannot assist you with business development. Test a variety of ways to cncourage referrals. You will learn from experience.

Referrals will not likely be made unless you show your sources what the advantages are. While it is obvious to you that everyone can benefit from referrals, others don't usually devote the effort unless prompted. You must find a professional way to communicate your desire to be the recipient of referrals. Some people are comfortable being rather direct in such matters. Others are not. If you are not comfortable, find a way to *subtly* communicate your interest. One professional takes time to explain, indirectly, how referrals are the lifeblood of her business. In essence, she plants the seed of suggestion and allows it to mature and bear fruit.

66. Promote Your Successes

Many of your satisfied clients lack the confidence in their ability to convey the importance of your worth to those to whom they recommend you. Communicating your value can be greatly enhanced through the use of external sources who can confirm your successes.

Concentrate all of your energy into building a public awareness of your talents. When many have great conviction about your abilities, this awareness reduces the anxiety that referral sources may have about their ability to judge your value.

Bonus tips:

1. Provide your clients (new and repeat) with a list of companies who value your service. Make available their addresses and phone numbers. Nothing breeds success like proving your past successes.
2. Have a list of testimonials on hand. Make sure that these testimonials are in the same fields of interest as your prospective clients. Include these testimonials and quotations in promotional materials and brochures. They are also powerful, as proof of your past performance, to include in price quotes, proposals, and estimates.

67. Make Sure Referral Sources Are Enthusiastic

To be effective, a referral has to be both compelling and enthusiastic. When motivating others to refer, you must create an almost religious zeal about your abilities, combined with an equal faith in your ethics, standards, and values. Work on strategies that promote this kind of support.

68. Prove That You're Worthy of Referrals

Referrals are made to those who are perceived as giving and not just taking. You should be perceived by others as a meaningful, contributing member of the profession, not just someone seeking to profit. Meaningful, generous, and significant contributions in the form of publishing information, participating in industry and/or professional educational and research endeavors, and assisting the less fortunate in ways appropriate to your abilities, help create an environment that encourages referrals.

69. Convince Referral Sources that Prospects Will Benefit More Than You Will

You receive referrals when sources believe that your services are uniquely suited to someone's needs. Therefore, your communications (letters, conversations, brochures, and other material) must be *specific* and *tailored*. Generalized communications are rarely productive. You must convince referring parties that you are the only one, or at least one of a handful of people, *especially* suited to the prospect's needs. Developing specialized communications is more time consuming, but it is worth the effort.

The referring party must perceive that the referral they make will benefit from your expertise as much as or more than you will benefit from getting their business. Valuable referrals are rarely made if the referring party feels you are in need or are indifferent about obtaining the business. Obviously, those who refer know in a general sense that you need business, but they must not think that the referral is critical to your survival. In your marketing efforts, you must convey that you are busy, successful, in demand, and have more opportunities presented to you than you can serve.

70. Uphold Ethical and Professional Standards

No matter how great your abilities and talents, people will not refer good business to you if they have any doubt about your ethics or professionalism. It is vital that you avoid any activity that detracts from your professional image. For example, never disclose information about clients or others that might be regarded as proprietary or confidential. And never engage in marketing practices that might cause others to question your ethics. The definition of ethical marketing behavior varies by field of specialization and is modified over time. But you are best to err on the side of caution.

71. Be Careful about Direct Solicitation

Unless you know that the potential referral source encourages you to do so, avoid soliciting directly for referrals or business. Direct solicitation may create the impression that you are needy or impoverished. It follows the idea of a television commercial: "Never let 'em see you sweat."

Instead, create an environment in which making a referral or directly engaging your services is *their* idea. You need to carefully strategize the relationship and the circumstances so that the potential referral will see it in their best interest to benefit you. In other words, let them think it was their idea to use your services.

72. Respond with Confidence to Requests for References

Expect and be prepared to respond to requests for references. If you look surprised and flustered, you will appear as though you lack experience and credibility. Instead, reach effortlessly into your attaché case and extract a long list of references. These should be people who have given you permission to be used as references, but they need not (all) be clients. There are many non-clients who can speak of your credibility, capacity, creativity, and character.

If prospective clients are constantly asking you for references before deciding to engage your services, you are insufficiently assertive, controlling, and directive. Prospects rarely ask for references unless you have failed to make them comfortable. References are not checked that often, anyway, and a request for references is often the prospect's way of avoiding a possible confrontation with you about his or her decision to decline the use of your services. If you are often asked for references, change your approach. It pays to experiment.

73. Create Silent Referrals through Written Reports

Develop the ability to obtain silent referrals. If your responsibilities include drafting final or interim reports, encourage the client to provide widespread circulation of your report. Develop a recommended circulation list, including a rationale for each distribution category. The very act of disseminating information creates a favorable image for you and serves as an unspoken referral.

Many projects provide no formal opportunity for you to show your involvement to outsiders or others who would benefit from this information. Encourage recognition of your involvement by proposing that you and the client (the most senior official with whom you have worked) draft a final report in the form of an article for a leading professional trade publication. Although jointly authored, you will probably do all the writing. When others see that your client thinks highly enough of you to jointly author a privately circulated research report, this knowledge will serve as a compelling endorsement to attract future business.

74. Circulate Tapes of Short Consultations

When you provide a short consultation for a client, consider taping the conversation and providing the client with a copy. The tape makes your services more beneficial because the client has a tangible product of your work together. Naturally, you must first request permission to tape the consultation.

Your client may want to share your tape with others, which can often lead to referral business. Some professionals have created information products (which they sell) that are based on excerpts from the tapes. If you do, please edit carefully to make sure that no confidential information is disclosed.

75. Be Careful When You Refer

Never refer a professional in whom you lack complete trust or confidence. One of the surest ways to hurt your own referral opportunities is to be seen as one who has questionable judgment or who makes unreliable recommendations.

If the person seeking referral from you keeps pressing, you can always provide him or her with several names of individuals who you understand claim to provide the desired service. State that you have no first-hand knowledge of their expertise or ethics. Be sure to let the person know that these names come with no endorsement and that he or she will have to satisfy himself with respect to their suitability.

76. Choose Gifts Wisely When Thanking Referral Sources

Devote careful thought and planning to the issue of giving gifts as rewards for providing referrals. A simple thank-you note should be promptly sent stating your appreciation and the potential benefits for the new client. A verbal thank-you is insufficient. A verbal thank-you followed by a written note of appreciation is much better. The advantage of a verbal thank-you is the immediate expression of appreciation.

You may also want to provide the referring source with a gift. Always keep in mind that a gift may be reviewed by the recipient as inappropriate, unethical, or unacceptable. Any gift should be selected with great care. Do not choose an expensive gift that may cause the recipient or others to question the nature of the gift. Choose a gift that is appropriate and that reflects the interests and tastes of the referring party.

Creativity in gift giving can have a significant impact on a generation of future referrals. For example, one highly regarded professional hosts a weekend twice a year at resorts, ski lodges, or hunting lodges. All expenses are paid and those invited to participate (about eight to 12 each time) are provided with two to three days of accommodations, food, spirits, and recreation. During these weekends, several hours are devoted to intellectual and professional pursuits tied closely to the host's expertise. These are enjoyable experiences that also benefit the host by providing an opportunity to share his latest creative ideas. The guests are exceptionally good clients, good potential sources of referrals, and others to whom the host feels a professional indebtedness.

Bonus tip: You do not always have to go to such great expenses as weekend retreats to have an impact on your clients. A simple gift reflecting the hobby or interest of a client can be appropriate and need not be expensive. A book in the client's field of interest would be a simple gift. You may also consider keeping several select, simple gourmet food items in your office as readily available gifts when the need arises.

77. Give Gifts at the Appropriate Time

Although it is extremely important to acknowledge and thank a referring party immediately in writing, the giving of a gift has its best impact at a *later* time. If you intend to send the gift especially in appreciation for a referral, then, by all means, send it immediately. However, a gift given at a later date is much more effective. An occasional remembrance acknowledging your appreciation of those who have helped you over the years may have a greater impact. The unexpected thank-you is remembered and appreciated more.

78. Don't Give Gifts Unless You Can Continue to do So

When selecting gifts to acknowledge the receipt of referrals, take care not to start something you will later be unable to continue. In other words, don't start something you can't finish. This is a good policy to follow for gift giving for any reason. One individual sent a tasteful and uncompromising gift after the receipt of one referral, but sent nothing in response to the second referral. The absence of the gift for the second referral stood out much more prominently. And another individual sent a nice Christmas gift for three years but reverted to sending just a card thereafter. Recipients wonder whether their business or referrals become less important or expected and thus unworthy of as meaningful an acknowledgement.

Chapter 6

Professional Speaking

79. Develop Public Speaking Now. *Immediately*

Nothing can boost your career like enhancing your talent and ability as a speaker. There are *hundreds* of speaking opportunities that can afford you the chance to reach hundreds of prospects for your services. Speaking is one of the very best ways to display your talents. So run, don't walk, to enroll in a Dale Carnegie course in your area. Thousands of business people, including former Chrysler chairman Lee Iacocca and several past U.S. Presidents rave about how Dale Carnegie training helped them.

Your local telephone directory lists dozens of associations, nonprofit organizations, service clubs, and self-help groups who are desperate for interesting speakers. Dale Carnegie training can teach you how to take your education, life experience, unique talents, and colorful personal stories, and package them so that audiences will flock to hear you. And in every audience there will be prospects eager to learn more about what you do and how it might benefit them.

To find out more about how the Dale Carnegie course can help you become a dynamic speaker, call the program's toll-free number: 1-800-231-5800. Tell the operator you are interested in "the original" Dale Carnegie course in public speaking and human relations. You'll be glad you did!

80. Get Out On the Stump

Knowing what to say and how to say it can turn an audience into clients. If you are saying the right *words* in the right *way*, to the right *group*, you may be able to turn many who hear you into viable prospects for your services. Orchestrate invitations to business, civic, professional, and technical groups that are comprised of potential clients and referral sources. Promote the availability of your speaking services to speakers' bureaus, associations, and corporate meeting planners.

Develop three or more short speeches that you can present to groups that would likely have prospective clients as members. When speaking, be sure to avoid a direct pitch. The audience did not come to hear your advertising. Be seen as knowledgeable, accessible, open, approachable, and receptive. But, rather than discuss your work at the podium, encourage those in the audience to pick up the phone and call you.

81. Invest in Your Speaking Career

You may have heard stories of professional speakers earning attractive honorariums of $1,000, $2,000, or even $5,000 a speech. And if the speaker is a movie star, television personality, or celebrity, then the sky's the limit as speaking fees go. While you may eventually position yourself to attract similar fees, you need to start with an "I," as in the word, "invest."

One of the tragic errors professionals make is trying to crack the speaking business without investing in their plan. Some of the key places you'll need to invest are:

1. *Speech classes.* From a Dale Carnegie course to a speech coach, to audio and video materials, invest in the business of speaking.
2. *Professional promotion materials.* Even if you are giving free speeches, invest in high quality materials that tell your story.
3. *Handouts.* With desktop publishing and quick printing, a small investment in workbooks and handouts can make you look like a real pro.
4. *Professional help.* From answering your phone to typing correspondence, go first class or stay at home.

82. Recognize that Professional Speaking Involves More than Just Opening Your Mouth

Many people may think that succeeding as a speaker is as simple as overcoming the *fear* of public speaking. While overcoming that fear is critical, there is much more to be learned if you plan to use professional speaking to reach prospects, remind clients, and build a referral reputation in your industry or profession.

To get started set up two notebooks, files, or file drawers. Label them:

- The Art of Speaking
- The Business of Speaking

Now you can begin to separate and catalog your research and reference material under these two broad headings.

Think of topic one—the *art* of speaking—as anything and everything that has to do with opening your mouth. It would cover professional speaking, from preparation to rehearsal, from delivery to after-action analysis. Start to keep a 24-hour search for ideas, articles, tips, and strategies to help you deliver *great* presentations.

The second area—the *business* of speaking—covers the areas of how to get bookings, communication with clients, setting fees, and so on. To insure that you get asked (or hired) to speak to your target groups become a proactive *marketer* of your skills.

Keep in mind that thousands of professionals are eager to speak, but are never asked. *Your* success will depend on hard work in both the art and the business of speaking. And most important, develop the knowledge, skills, attitudes, and habits of a speaking professional.

83. Improve Your Skill with Each Speaking Engagement

If you speak for two years or twenty, these three types of speeches will haunt you:

First, there is the speech you *plan* to give, the speech you research, and the speech you plan and rehearse again and again.

Second, there is the speech you *gave*. And unless you are following a boring word-for-word script, you are certain to have deviated, improvised and perhaps, added some spontaneous comments.

Third, there is the speech you *wish* you had given. After your speech, those "after-the-fact flashes" are certain to haunt you. It is 100% normal to kick yourself for some things you said, and for some things you wish you had said.

The lesson learned:

> Although every good speaker works to close the gap between these three categories, learn to loosen up and *grow* from *each* speaking engagement.
>
> Ask yourself these two questions:

1. "Next time I speak, what do I want to *say* differently?" Keep a diary, journal, or notebook—and review your notes just prior to your next engagement.
2. "Next time I speak, what do I want to *do* differently?" Record details about logistics—everything from changing the room temperature to handling handouts.

84. Be a Proactive Speaker

Meeting planners and coordinators will form a strong opinion of you as you work with them to arrange the details for speaking to their groups. If you are polished and proactive, you'll rush the materials they need—often before they need them. But if getting what they need means hounding, repeating phone calls, and pleading with you to follow through, the planners' negative opinion of you can be *deadly* to your professional image. It can destroy the reputation you are striving to build through your speaking efforts.

Start today to put together a resource file, complete with a checklist that will allow you to rush materials to such contacts.

Here are some of the basic items you'll need almost every time:

- A black-and-white three-by-five-inch photo of yourself
- Your biography
- Promotion copy (minimum of one paragraph) about your topic
- Room arrangement or layout diagram
- A list of audio-visual requirements, such as slide projectors and flip charts
- A typed, official introduction covering your background and/ or your topic

Bonus tip: As requests are received for materials, expand your resource file and your materials checklist. Soon everything you need will be at your fingertips.

85. Write Your Own Opening and Closing Remarks

When being introduced before a speech or participation in a panel discussion, draft your own introduction and provide it to the host. Indicate that the host may use the introduction or not, but that others have found the material useful for organizing introductory remarks.

Don't make your introduction too lengthy. Provide it on a small, unobtrusive piece of paper and use type of sufficient size that it will be easy to read. Write it in newspaper (inverted pyramid) style, putting the most important information first and the less important information later, although it should close on an important high. Doing so permits you to control, or at least influence, what is said about you and how it is said.

When it is comfortable and appropriate, write a closing for the host, acknowledging the remarks that you made. Many hosts fumble for appropriate words to say at the close. You will make them more comfortable and be able to communicate the kind of information that will lead to increased referral and business opportunities.

86. Use Personal Anecdotes to Add Interest to Your Speeches

When flying to paid speaking engagements, the most important item one consultant packs is a worn green plastic file folder labeled "JW's Gems." The folder contains a treasury of personal stories, anecdotes, experiences and proven strategies to share with audiences. The consultant considers the folder so valuable, that he keeps a backup copy at home in a fireproof file. Here's why:

The best material to share are those things you've *personally* lived—the lessons learned from your thrills of victory and agonies of defeat, your wisdom or triumphs, your tribulations and temptations. Sharing your own library of material means you can tell colorful material with a passion. You can make these colorful stories and experiences come alive as you rekindle the step-by-step details to share with your audience. Remember, *you* are the number one world's best authority on you and what you think.

Start you own "gems" file today. Begin a file of possible speech material as you live life's twists and quirks.

Here is a simple and quick way to catalog your material:

- Customer Service—first impressions—"Old Inn Story". . . smile big as Texas.
- Menu reader boards in Japan—"Smiles, Zero Yen"
- Shoe Repair Shop—"Our customers are happy because I'm not."

The first example is a code to recount an unusual dining experience used to drive home a reminder about the old adage, "You never get a second chance to make a good first impression."

Start your own "gems" file *now.*

87. Use Showmanship to *Be Remembered*

One of today's greatest challenges is getting attention and being remembered in a hectic, overcommunicated, and fiercely competitive market. Consider adding a touch of showmanship and fun to make clients remember your presentations (whether they are sales presentations, training sessions, or progress reports).

For example, when faced with a critical turnaround at a Western wholesale distributor, one consulting firm handed out fresh lemons to company's 50-plus managers who were attending a hastily called conference. After a brief discussion about the lemons (symbolic of their company's near bankruptcy), the consultants made one key point: the only way to make 100% pure, fresh, hand-squeezed lemonade is to have lemons. And for this group, there was only one choice—to make lemonade from the managers' lemons.

Think about creative and unique graphics you can use to convey a point and at the same time be remembered. Here are some ideas to help you start your own creative approach:

- Take a pie and cut it up to demonstrate how your audience can gain a bigger piece of the pie.
- Give a stuffed alligator to demonstrate a new aggressiveness from your sales training.
- Use piles of play money to show how your accounting work will boost cash flow.

Look around . . . let your mind wander . . . ideas are everywhere to help you be remembered.

88. Do a "SALT" Check on Every Meeting Room's Equipment

One of your strategic "make or break" areas as a speaker is the status of the room in which you will speak. If things are going your way and are nearly perfect, you'll probably do exceptionally well. And if things are in chaos—from a terrible seating arrangement to a near-boiling temperature, from poor lighting to a crackling sound system—you are headed for a disaster, frequently called "bombing" among professionals.

When making a speech or presentation, check out and arrange the facilities and equipment in advance of your talk. Check the microphone or slide projector, and determine whether there is a glass of water on the podium—these are not tasks that should be done after you have been introduced.

Remember: prospects are watching you and you want them to perceive you as the professional's professional.

Avoid future disasters by doing a SALT check on every meeting room. SALT is an acronym that reminds you to check the following items:

S *Seating.* Arrive early and, whenever possible, rearrange the seating to best fit your style.

A *Audio.* Check and recheck the sound system before your audience arrives. Ask for and use the professional help offered by many meeting facilities. And when you know that everything is perfect in the audio department, guard it like a mother hen.

L *Lights.* Remember that for most presentations, it is best to have all lights on and adjusted up to their maximum. Good lighting makes it easier for the audience to see you and any props, marker boards, and flip charts. Besides, ever try to sleep with bright lights glaring in your eyes?

T *Temperature.* Sure the room feels great now, but add 50 hot bodies and where will it be? Err on the side of being cool. Estimate how much air-conditioning will be required to offset your audience's combined body temperatures.

Remember, when setting up your speaking environment, just pass the SALT.

89. Speak Up!

How many times have you tried to hear speakers, but no matter how hard you tried, they just weren't audible? Here is a rule that will eliminate this disaster for you:

Always talk to the person *farthest away* from you. For example, if you have 30 rows in your audience, forget the first 29 rows and use your voice to reach the last person in that last row. Because speakers' ears are just six inches from their mouths, all too often they fail to realize that most of the audience can't hear them. And nothing destroys your professionalism like not being heard.

When speaking in hotels, conference rooms, churches, and similar public facilities, take advantage of their sound systems and microphones. Amateur speakers often shy away from sound equipment—and these speakers are the ones who need it most.

Bonus tip: If you have *any* concerns about your voice volume level, position a room monitor or two in the back corners of the room. Ask your monitors to give you a "thumbs up" or "thumbs down" when you need to adjust your voice level. Also ask them to give you the "OK" or "right on" target signal when they can hear you comfortably.

90. Listen to Yourself and Learn

Nothing can make a speaker more humbler than hearing one of his or her own presentations, or reading a word-for-word transcript of a speech just given. At the same time, there is no better way to learn than to carefully dissect every talk you give.

Follow these suggestions:

1. *Tape every talk you give.* Invest in a good standard or micro-cassette recorder.
2. *Don't worry about capturing "broadcast quality" recordings.* Just focus on "good enough." That is, get a recording of good-enough quality that you can relive the presentation (without the pressure and stress of a live program).
3. *Keep notes on the changes you want to make the next time you speak.* Consider how you can power up a story, add more color to your examples, and deliver your humor with more punch.
4. *Listen for what you are doing well.* Recognize that you did some things exceptionally well and build on those positives. Give yourself some pats on the back.
5. *Going from average, to good, to great can take years of hard work.* Stay with these steps, and you'll be great in less time than even you can imagine.

CHAPTER 7

Media Contacts and Public Relations

91. Write Articles for Trade Magazines

"Extra, extra, read all about it!" Make sure your name and ideas are published in the leading trade magazines that are seen by your clients on a regular basis. Here's how:

1. Comment on what important persons in the field are saying.
2. Interpret general news and how it will impact your clients.
3. Develop and report on surveys you conduct.
4. Provide articles of informational value—with a lead to request additional information.

The more often your name and ideas are seen by your *prospects*, the more likely they will become your *clients*. Working the press on a consistent basis is *vital* for your professional exposure and future business. You are seen as a leading expert in your field. What your clients read and hear about you through this process is much more effective than just plain advertising.

The strategies discussed in this chapter are designed to make sure that you deal with the press effectively. For example, when sending a press release, always include a photo. Doing so increases the probability that your press release will be printed. If you plan to use a photo of yourself in marketing materials or publicity campaigns, use a *professional* photographer who specializes in "executive portraiture." This is *not* the time to save money with inexpensive home photography. A poor photo can do more harm than good.

92. Recognize that the Press Does Not Owe You any Coverage

Many professionals seeking publicity communicate an attitude that the press owes them coverage. Nothing could be further from the truth. And such an attitude could be extremely detrimental to your efforts to obtain press coverage.

Obvious? Of course! But consider this: In a rush to get publicity, you see others who have equally or even less worthy causes than yours who seem to receive considerable coverage. You may then maintain the attitude that "I *deserve* to be covered." And no matter how subtly you convey it, it will hurt you.

The business of the media is to provide news and information that are of value to its audiences. With so much to choose from, the media has great latitude in determining who and what will be covered. Publicity for you is *elective*—which means that the *attitude* you communicate about the media and the individuals you deal with have a great impact on your success. The media is not an extension of your marketing department. Its representatives owe you nothing. If you have information of value that attracts their attention, you may be fortunate enough to benefit by receiving publicity. Don't forget this: press coverage is a *privilege*, not a right.

93. Don't Waste the Valuable Time of the Media with Unimportant Trivia

The majority of news releases never receive coverage by the media. There are many reasons why a release isn't provided coverage, of course, but none more pervasive than the fact that the release deals with *unimportant information*.

Most professionals send out three press releases during their entire career. The first announces the fact that they have started practice, the second communicates the fact that they have removed themselves to larger offices, and the third broadcasts their retirement. Failing to see their names in print, they conclude that obtaining publicity is an unproductive effort.

They failed to receive coverage for a simple reason. Starting practice, moving a practice and retiring are not news—very few people care. If you are located in a small town where the local newspaper feels an obligation to report on any and all local business happenings, you might get a line or two of ink. But in a major market, there is far more important news worthy of the very limited space available. Of course, a highly specialized industry or professional newsletter may provide coverage, but even this isn't too likely.

If you want publicity, you must come up with information that is truly of interest. If you are unable or unwilling to do so, don't waste your time or that of the representatives of the media.

94. Generate Real News

Generating news and information of sufficient value that will be worthy of serious consideration by the press is easy.

Start by doing something that a great many journalists do—ask the question: "What information would be of value and interest for the audience I am attempting to communicate with?" Asking this question gives you *focus* and *direction*. It's a proven principle of target marketing.

True marketers may not be always right, but they do target. That is, they begin by considering their market. The market is defined as readers of a publication, a mailing list of an association, or other select groups. Marketers ask the question, "What would these readers be interested in buying?" They *tailor* a product to the market they are trying to penetrate.

This same principle can be applied to publicity efforts. If you ask about the audience's interests, you can generate news that has a high probability of attracting the interest of the media aimed at that audience.

One way to ask is to conduct research on a provocative question and report on your findings. For example, when scheduling a seminar in a city, publicizing that fact will create additional registrations. But the decision to conduct a seminar isn't newsworthy. However, a press release comparing local and national averages for consultant and professional fees or business prospects might be. More media coverage may be devoted to a *researcher* who is discussing these *trends* than to a consultant who is promoting his seminar.

You may feel that collecting research data is difficult, time consuming, or costly. Certainly it can be, but not always. A small survey of attitudes or opinions may not qualify for a doctoral dissertation, but it can provide interesting insight that will attract the attention of the media—because the information is of interest to the audiences they are trying to reach.

95. Don't Write the Same Pitch Over and Over Again

Everyone has been hooked by the notion that it is efficient to do something one time, then magnify the effort by reproducing it over and over again. While this is *efficient*, it may not be *effective* when generating publicity. Most people seeking publicity—including a high percentage of professional publicists—create a general press release, make multiple copies and mail it to every potential press lead they can unearth.

You will be far more successful if you *avoid* this practice and concentrate on *tailoring* your publicity to the *unique interest* of each potential lead. Perhaps even better—don't send a release at all. Instead, write a personal letter that communicates on a *personal* level, which will motivate the recipient to more carefully consider the value of providing publicity for your endeavor.

As with marketing publicity, efforts need to be targeted. While it is far more time consuming to prepare a specific *targeted* communication, try concentrating on obtaining publicity for a smaller *select* segment of the media. In marketing and publicity, the key is to focus on a select group that you want to reach.

96. Seize Opportunities to Create More Media Coverage

Those who are good at getting publicity seem to have a sense for opportunity that everyone should work at developing. A good question to ask regularly: "Is there a new publicity angle to what I am doing?"

For example, one professional presented a three-hour workshop to a group of consultants at a national professional association meeting. The workshop followed a keynote luncheon speech by no less than the chairman of the President's Council of Economic Advisors. The speaker took questions following his address. He was asked many. Several consultants wanted to know what he thought about the economy for the consulting profession in the months ahead.

During the workshop the consultant saw an opportunity to build on the keynote speech: He taught the consultants who had been present at the keynote how to turn the keynote speech into a publicity event that would benefit them. If someone had asked a question about the future of the economy relative to the interests of the clients and industry he or she served, that consultant could have developed a news release detailing an "interview" with the chairman of the President's Council of Economic Advisors. Then that release could be distributed to the trade press to be read by clients and prospects. The probability of receiving coverage for such news was quite high. Therefore, that consultant could have used an ordinary keynote speech as an opportunity for personal media coverage.

Further, the opportunity also existed to retain a photographer to have a picture taken with the keynote speaker. Government officials are willing and eager to participate in such photo sessions. Such a photo could be sent with the press release.

97. Be Creative—and Controversial—When Seeking Media Coverage

Opportunities present themselves almost daily that can be turned to publicity advantage if you take more time to be creative.

For example, when reading a trade publication (or even the general media), you will see remarks made by colleagues or competitors with which you agree or disagree. It is often a good idea for you to draft a press release refuting or supporting such opinions. This media tends to like *controversy*—so by disagreeing, you maintain a more powerful position. And the more important the person you are refuting or the more controversial you appear, the more likely your effort will produce coverage.

It's okay to be somewhat controversial. Some fear that doing so will hurt business opportunities. But since it is unlikely that you will be able to do business with everyone, it will be beneficial for you to cause the market to have mixed emotions. If half of your market feels you are a raving maniac, but the other half feels you walk on water, controversy may be to your benefit.

98. Don't Forget to Thank Media Professionals for the Publicity They've Generated

Many who are fortunate enough to receive the favorable publicity they have worked so hard to obtain never take the time to say "thank you." It is simple, common courtesy to thank those who have done something that benefits you. Because so few say "thanks," the fact that you do will more likely be remembered and could benefit your publicity efforts later.

When thanking a member of the press for publicity, it is best to make the expression of gratitude helpful and meaningful. This does *not* mean sending a gift. Never do anything that would cause the individual, the publisher, or others to think that the editorial integrity of the journalist has in any way been compromised.

What, then, constitutes a "helpful and meaningful" expression of gratitude? Ask yourself a simple question: "If I were this person, what information would I find of value to receive?" The answer may take many forms.

For example, as a result of newspaper publicity about one of a consultant's booklets, he received several hundred responses. He concluded that the columnist would probably have an interest in knowing something about the nature of the respondents. Most writers want to know who reads and who responds to a particular item. The consultant analyzed the respondents by such factors as profession, geographic location, and gender. He then forwarded this information to the columnist, along with a letter expressing his appreciation for the publicity.

99. Make Media Relations a Two-Way Street

In addition to always taking the time and trouble to thank your media contacts for publicity received, it will be in your interest to expend effort on a regular basis to develop a reciprocal relationship with members of the media.

Most professionals seeking publicity won't bother to develop helpful relationships. So if you do, you are more likely to be noticed and remembered. Make it a policy to communicate two or three times each year (and more often, if possible) with your media contacts in a way that is other than self-serving. As you pick up information, hear about research, and run into useful data, ask yourself this question: "Which individuals on my media contact list would find this information of value?"

Then communicate it to them. If you run into an interesting story idea that you feel would be of value, tell them.

Look at it this way: If you were a member of the press who only heard from consultants when you could benefit them, you might be less responsive than if you received a variety of communications—including some that solely benefited your own career.

100. Understand That You Can't Buy the Legitimate Press

Even in this enlightened age there are some who feel that they can *buy* good press coverage. They believe that since they have spent or offered to spend "significant" sums on advertising, they *deserve* editorial coverage.

Sometimes they are right. There *are* some publications that quite regularly trade editorial coverage for advertising. But the legitimate, respected press does not. What makes publicity so effective for those who receive it is the *editorial integrity* of the publication. Generally speaking, the more highly respected a publication, the greater its editorial integrity. Knowing this, the legitimate press takes great pains to ensure that its integrity is never compromised.

When available, you may find it advantageous to benefit from publicity made available in exchange for advertising or other commercial benefit. But, take care that you never approach the legitimate press with an exchange attitude. Doing so will be very damaging to your prospects for obtaining publicity and to your general image with the media.

101. Pay Attention to Details When Contacting Media Professionals

When the daily mail arrives, you likely pay far more attention to letters that are addressed to you by name, properly spelled, specifying your correct position, title, and address. So do members of the media. While it is easier to fire off press releases to "Business Editor, *Chicago Tribune*," it may only gain attention equal to the attention you devote to your own "Resident" or "Occupant" mail.

Just as your communications with the media will do better if they are specific and targeted to the special interests and concerns of the recipient, it is important that you invest time and effort on the *details*:

- Write to people by name.
- Be sure the spelling of their name and publication is correct.
- Do the research necessary to ensure that you are reaching the one person at the publication or broadcast station who has the *greatest* interest in your cause.
- Check job titles, professional or academic designations, and addresses with great care.

Any major library has a variety of media directories that will help you check these facts. But directories get out of date quickly. *Confirm* information by telephone and update your records *regularly*.

We all get busy and look for shortcuts. But ask yourself this question: "If I fail to get publicity because I created a poor image by misspelling a journalist's name, did I make a wise decision about my priorities?"

102. Consider Using Public Relations Professionals

If your publicity effort is unique and highly newsworthy, and if you want to make an impact on a narrow group of specialized trade magazines, then you may be able to get good results on your own. But if you are trying to impact major-market mass media or obtain publicity in a crowded, competitive niche market, you may be frustrated by your lack of success. You may surmise that a public relations professional could generate significantly greater impact.

Generally, the more difficult your publicity objective, the more you will benefit from the services of experienced, creative professionals. There are three advantages to using skilled public relations professionals:

1. *Contacts.* A good professional has done or knows how to do the necessary research (fairly quickly) to identify the best media contacts.
2. *Influence.* Most members of the press come to rely on professionals to bring them information and news. If a press member knows that 70% of the time a particular publicist can be depended upon to bring a good story lead, the journalist is more likely to respond to that publicist's communications than to the stack of unsolicited press releases on the desks.
3. *Creativity.* Professional publicists are often imaginative and creative. They often know how to package an idea or make an image appeal to the media.

You *can* do this yourself; even the most difficult publicity objectives can be accomplished without professional assistance. Doing so, however, requires that you master the tools used by professionals and learn the tricks of the trade. You need to ask yourself, "Do I have the time to become proficient at generating desirable coverage?"

As with most things, when buying professional services, you get what you pay for. Most publicity professionals charge either on a project basis or on a monthly retainer. The fees are expensive. And, you are responsible for their direct expenses, which can be considerable. In seeking their services, you are likely to be quoted a variety of fees. Evaluate the candidates' approaches, their ideas, and styles—and then make your decision accordingly.

103. Plan Ahead to Handle Response to Your PR Campaign

Don't begin efforts to generate publicity until you have carefully considered how to handle the response if your efforts are successful.

Do you have time to be responsive? What if 30 writers want to interview you? Suppose 16 local A.M. television talk shows want you to be a guest? How would you handle 7,321 mail-in requests for information? The time to think about handling the results of your publicity effort is *before* you start—not after you achieve the desired result.

The publicity you create will be wasted unless you are able to respond *quickly* and *appropriately*. Before you pitch the bookers, producers, or hosts of all the local television talk shows, ask yourself if you are willing to travel all over the country, *at your own expense*, to do five-minute segments at the drop of a hat.

Do you have adequate staff support to quickly process hundreds or thousands of requests for information? Be prepared. If not, the publicity will become a burden rather than a benefit.

104. Always, *Always* Make Time for the Press!

Response to your publicity efforts seem to arrive at the most inconvenient times. Writers call a few minutes or a few hours before deadline. Guests scheduled for talk and interview shows cancel at the last minute, creating an opening that the producer hopes *you* can fill.

To maximize the results of your publicity-seeking efforts, you must *always* make time for the press, be *immediately* responsive, follow-up *quickly*, and work at *their* convenience, not your own.

When called for a quote, interview, comment or information, stop whatever you are doing and respond at the time. If you absolutely *can't* respond at the moment, inquire about deadline and schedule, then respond as quickly as necessary. When a good live appearance opportunity comes about, change your schedule and plan to be there.

Just like you, members of the press wait for the last minute and are motivated by deadlines. Be responsive to their schedules. *Follow-up immediately.* When they need information, be prepared to fax it instantly or send it by overnight mail, if necessary.

Make sure that you are viewed by your media contacts as being instantly available, immediately responsive, and sensitive to their needs.

105. Try to Get Your Address and Phone Number Included in All Media Mentions

Publicity is wonderful—but publicity that includes your address and phone number is almost a sure trip to the bank. When dealing with the media, be creative in coming up with angles that are likely to result in having your address and phone number included in the press you receive.

Remember, people are often a little lazy. If it's convenient to get in touch with you, they will. If not, most won't bother. If people are really interested in reaching you, they could always contact the media to get your address or phone number. But again, most don't go to the trouble. By the time they get your phone number, some may not remember why they wanted it in the first place.

Agreeing to provide free or low-cost information is an excellent device for getting your address and phone number published. Professionals are frequently interviewed by newspaper and magazine writers who ask questions related to their practices, research, and fees. At some point during the interview, a professional may say something like, "By the way, if any of your readers would like a complete summary of the data, I would be happy to provide it to them without charge. All they need is to write or phone and request it."

If you are doing a broadcast interview, you can make a similar statement. The interviewer then has little choice but to ask for your phone number and address to permit the audience to take advantage of your gracious generosity.

There is great value in encouraging the media to provide information on how to contact you. A newspaper columnist wrote two articles that included information about a consultant and his ideas. In one article, it was mentioned that the consultant's booklets were available at $3 plus sales tax and his address was given. The publicity resulted in *more than 450 individuals ordering the booklet*. In the other article no mention was made of the booklet, and no information was included on how to contact me.

Only a few readers went to the trouble of figuring out how to get in touch.

The fact that only a few spent the effort to get in touch doesn't mean the publicity wasn't effective. Much of the benefit of publicity is indirect. The more favorable publicity you receive, the more your image is enhanced, and the more effective your indirect and direct marketing will be in the future. *Always* look for an easy way for the audience to get in touch with you.

106. Respond to Publicity-Generated Leads Immediately!

You probably receive sales literature in the mail and sometimes wonder why it was sent to you. If you reflect for a few moments, you may remember that several weeks earlier you had an interest and requested it. A cold lead is a dead lead.

If you are going to the effort and expense to obtain publicity, be sure to respond to the leads *promptly*. We live in a society of instant gratification. If you need a carton of milk at 1:00 A.M. you can go to the local convenience store. If you want a photocopy at 3:00 A.M. you can go to the local all-night copy center. People don't like to wait for anything—and they don't have to. If you are unable or unwilling to respond immediately, your competition can and will.

Respond to leads received the very day, or at worst the next day. Get to them while they are hot. Interest wanes *fast*. And usually when people request information, they are requesting it from several sources. The first to respond has the greatest chance of getting the business.

Living by such a policy has resulted in much business and good will in many businesses. Someone may call at 5:15 P.M. and request information. A personal letter and sales literature are mailed that evening. In the local area, it is likely to be delivered by noon the next day. The prospect frequently calls to do business and almost always comments on the speed of response and the quality of service.

107. Aim Your Publicity to Get *Qualified* Leads

Just getting leads may not be productive. Not all leads are business opportunities. What you really want are *qualified* leads, of course. Your publicity efforts should be directed toward ensuring that you acquire leads with the right potential.

Many years ago, inflight magazine publishers discovered the reader response card. Since you could not telephone from an airplane in those days to order or request information, and since you probably were not inclined to write a letter while aloft, these cards were a great device. People could take a pencil and circle numbers, mail the card after disembarking, and receive information. The concept has become popular for almost all magazines.

Some advertisers realized that when the air is thin, and the liquor is flowing, and people have little to occupy their minds, some travelers become mesmerized by the response cards and circle those little numbers aimlessly. As a result, they received mountains of information, but few bought. Indeed, some advertisers began to request that they be left off the response cards. Responding to the leads was too costly for the business obtained.

In seeking publicity, if you are not too discriminating, you can get lots of leads. But are they the right leads? *Screen* publicity opportunities to ensure that you get qualified leads. When making information offers, consider charging a dollar or two as a means of separating the interested from those who just like to receive mail.

108. Be Creative in Your Public Relations Efforts

Direct marketers expend great effort figuring out how to get your attention. With the mountains of promotional solicitations received these days and the busy schedules everyone keeps, they know that they have to be creative to have their promotional message noticed.

Since you are but one of hundreds or thousands contacting the media to gain publicity, it will be in your interest to think like the most creative direct marketers. No, the press has not seen everything. *Creativity pays off.* Anything that you can do, in good taste, to encourage your pitch for publicity to be noticed and responded to as you desire will be beneficial.

Some writers on the subject of publicity and public relations advise that all interactions with the media be in ways only proven *by tradition.* Often this practice is good, but be careful that you don't follow tradition so closely that your communications to the media are ignored. Members of the press are impacted by many of the same changes as their readers. This fact sometimes permits you to depart from the way things have always been done. It is better to receive coverage than to adhere strictly to tradition.

109. Use Press Coverage to Get *More* Press Coverage

The more coverage you receive from the press, the more you will receive. If you, your product, your project, or your cause are to become "household" words, you want as much favorable press as possible. And getting press is one of the best ways to get *more* press.

You may have noticed that certain sources seem to be quoted repeatedly. They are not only frequently mentioned in a given publication, but in the media in general. Here's why:

Most journalists keep a file or notebook of sources by subject matter. When working on a story, they turn to the appropriate file. If you are there, you will likely get a call and be asked for your opinion or information. If there is no one under the category or an insufficient number of sources, the reporter is likely to take a look at other articles on the subject. If you were mentioned or quoted there, you are likely to get a call. The more files and notebooks you can find your way into, the more media coverage you can anticipate.

Simply put—press begets press!

110. Write Controversial Letters to the Editor

Read the publications produced by your press contacts and note items with which you agree and disagree. Draft press releases as suggested previously (page 106), or letters to the editor, as appropriate, to state the nature of your agreement or disagreement and forward them to the publications. Not all will be published, but many will. Those in a position to refer or make use of your services directly will begin to notice, over time, that your thinking is of sufficient value that it is regularly picked up or communicated by the press. The publicity increases your value in the minds of prospects and referral sources, and they will have greater confidence in your services.

111. Be Seen as a Knowledgeable Interpreter of Events in Your Industry

Interpret important events and communications for those in a position to use your services directly or to refer business. One of the greatest benefits a professional can provide is the ability to interpret information from the general environment and point out its strategic significance to those in a narrower field of specialty.

Review or analyze important news and business events and statements of important individuals such as business, economic, and political leaders. Then interpret such information for its importance to those in your market. Communicate this information in the form of press releases and/or letters to the editor.

CHAPTER 8

Distributing Information Products

112. Write Brochures that Arouse the Prospect's Curiosity

When developing capability statements or brochures describing your services, don't get too lengthy or detailed. A good brochure should raise as many questions as it answers because "Inquiring minds want to know." The purpose of these marketing tools is to get the prospect to *contact* you, not to provide a reference of your services. Disclosing all the details only removes the need to obtain more information by talking with you.

You also want to create curiosity around the subject matter, which motivates the client to ask for more information. For example, one marketing brochure refers to such subtopics as, "My dog is a salesman, too." In other words, an itemized list of your services and a dry discussion of the subject matter only eliminate the need for further contact.

One educational consulting firm learned this lesson when it published a 36-page brochure that described every service it could offer. The consultants were surprised to find their response to the mailing was poor. Their next brochure was designed to raise more questions than answers. It invited readers to communicate their need for more information. The response, which came from the same mailing list, was almost four times as great!

113. Test Every Marketing Communication

Every marketing communication that you write should be tested to be sure that it communicates in the way intended. Give your writing to at least three people and ask them to tell you what it says to them and how they perceive the person or firm who would write it. Don't give it to people who wouldn't want to hurt your feelings—they won't really be frank. Give it to those who could care less about hurting your feelings.

When you write a sales letter, brochure, or advertisement for your services, *always* check it for *readability*. Either use a reading-level measure or put what you have written in the hands of a 13-year-old child who reads on grade level and ask that child to tell you, in his own words, what you have said. You may be surprised to find that you communicate on a level that requires someone to read beyond the level necessary to read the morning paper. You shouldn't. *It will cost you clients.*

Take care that all written communications are well written, with correct usage, grammar, and spelling. Poorly written communications detract from referral opportunities. If you have weaknesses, harness human or computer resources to clean up and clarify your writing.

114. Show Clients the Value of Your Free Information Products

If you've authored a book, audiotape, or video, or produced other educational items, then you are well acquainted with the term, "freebie." You've probably handed out and mailed more free material than you care to discuss. Now you can get extra value and boost the perception of the materials you give away to promote your business.

Resolve today that all such free materials, especially those sent to prospects and clients, will be accompanied by an itemized invoice. Show line by line the value of the items—including freight. Next, purchase a large rubber stamp for just this occasion and enclose the itemized invoice with the word, "Complimentary," stamped in big, red letters.

With this simple system you can change something from a freebie to something with specific value. For example, it's not just a book, it is $33.95. It makes a tremendous impact: You get a bigger bang for your buck.

115. Prequalify Your Leads

Advertising professional services *directly* is usually not productive. You can achieve better results if you develop an information product—perhaps a booklet—that prospects will request. This product will serve as a *screening* device by which you can prequalify your leads.

Response to advertisements for information products can produce more leads than a direct pitch to engage your services.

By charging a nominal fee (such as $1 to $5) for an information product, you set up the expectation to pay for the information you have made available.

Free advice is rarely taken. But if you have to pay someone for it, you pay attention. A dollar amount increases a product's value. Try developing and promoting an information product and charging a small fee for it. Frequently, it produces a better-qualified lead. Those unwilling to pay a nominal fee for information will probably not pay your fee anyway.

Of course, the fee should not prevent you from giving this information to others at no cost. With the value designated on the report, the individual who received the report at no cost will recognize its significance as well as those who paid. Greater attention will be paid to the information.

But be careful: most people do not like to pay for advertising material only. Make sure the product communicates valuable and important *information* that is beneficial. Keep the self-promotion tasteful.

Instead of sending the information products out to all your prospects, consider sending a letter with a P.S. stating that it is available at a nominal fee. This qualifier separates your serious clients from those who are looking for freebies.

116. Set a Fair Price for Your Information Products

When creating new products—from writing a small pamphlet to authoring a complex cassette learning program—don't be afraid to ask a fair (substantial) price for your products. This rule is especially true for very specialized and niche-oriented items that people can't buy anywhere else.

Don't ever forget that you *aren't* selling books, tapes, and printed products . . . you are selling *information*. Better yet, if you have done proper research and homework, you are offering a one-of-a-kind information package that you can term "proprietary information."

Consider how drug companies, inventors, and holders of patents and trademarks collect for their unique and often exclusive products and services.

One word of caution . . . we are talking about *a fair and equitable pricing strategy*—not ripping off clients. Do some homework by asking a number of prospective buyers what they perceive to be a fair price for your new product. Ask them to give you a high-to-low scale of pricing variables. It won't take long for them to help you plot a selling price. And most of the time, you'll be surprised that their price is considerably *more* than you imagined you might get.

117. Don't Price Products like Services

Increasingly, professionals are developing information products, such as computer software, manuals, and audio tapes. Indeed, the products represent a major trend in the delivery of professional services. Be careful. Don't price products like services. If the work you do for a client is really a product or customized product (something that can easily be replicated for future clients), it is not in your interest to collect the development cost from each individual client. Doing so makes you noncompetitive. If development takes 80 hours and you expect to sell the product ten times, add eight hours of development time as the cost to each client.

Do not worry that creating an information product will hurt your chances to sell your services. Properly developed and marketed, such information products *stimulate* a demand for your services. The information product produces a profit in its own right, and becomes a powerful promotional avenue for your services.

Frequently prospects who have read your materials, or saw or heard an audio- or videotape are often captivated by their learning experience. Many will want to hire you to help them implement the approach you spoke or wrote about.

118. Don't Be Too Pushy When Distributing Promotional Material

Avoid pushing volumes of promotional materials on prospects and referral sources. Doing so may give you the appearance of being needy and hungry. Also, those who benefit the most from the information are those who request it.

For example, if you are participating in a panel discussion at an association meeting, bury the motivation to place in each participant's hand a copy of your promotional brochures. Instead, when making remarks, describe the *value* of the information you have available. Encourage participants to give you their business cards so that you may send a brochure *later*. This practice will avoid the appearance that you are inappropriately anxious for business. It also provides you with the opportunity to follow up *personally* with each interested individual.

119. Avoid Setting Out a Stack of Your Brochures

When speaking before a group, avoid setting out a stack of your brochures (capability statements) for the audience members to pick up and read. Instead, during your talk, mention a valuable information product or item that you will be pleased to send if they will give you a business card. The cards permit you to follow up *personally* with each audience member—and to add his or her name to your mailing list for future contact. Just as you are concluding your remarks, remind the audience members to leave their business cards if they want the free copy of whatever you've described.

As an added benefit, your host or sponsor will see the group so motivated by your words that people rush up and surround you when you have finished speaking. This obvious interest increases the probability that you will be asked to speak again.

Chapter 9

Preparing Contracts

120. Don't Look at Proposal Writing as a Burden

Don't look upon writing a proposal as unnecessary drudgery for getting the business. Even when the client does not require a proposal, you should usually take the initiative in developing one. Those who write proposals (even when they don't have to) may wind up with *bigger and better assignments*. Those who write proposals most of the time probably have annual incomes that are higher than those who only write proposals occasionally. And, a *well-written* proposal may result in a bigger, more comprehensive assignment. The proposal identifies a broader scope of work than may first be obvious.

Develop proposal-writing skills that are right for marketing your services. The kind of proposal that you must write to get the business is different from most proposals. Your proposal is unique. It is designed *to get business*. If you learned your proposal-writing skills within an organization where proposals were primarily designed *to inform*, you are probably writing the wrong kind of proposal. It will cost you in *lost business*.

When selling your services face-to-face, in a letter, or in a formal proposal, don't communicate how you will provide the desired results in such detail that you can provide the client with a recipe. Doing so removes the need for retaining you.

If you have developed a proposal that fails to gain a new client, identify who else would benefit from such services and recycle your proposal to others.

When following up on a proposal or sales call, don't call to ask if the prospect is ready to give you the business. Doing so gives the impression that you are hungry and needy. Instead, find a tangible reason to communicate with the prospect—such as new information, or an event in the industry about which the prospect may not be familiar, and use that knowledge as a rationale for calling.

121. *Always* Use a Written Agreement

Always, always, *always* work with a written contract or agreement. It need not be overly formal or read as if it requires a committee of lawyers to interpret. A simple letter of understanding is often sufficient. Such a document clarifies communications, expectations, and responsibilities and is invaluable should a misunderstanding or dispute ever occur.

Develop and have ready to use several stock agreements that are appropriate for the clients you serve and the services you provide. These can be quickly modified as needed. Written agreements arc a mark of a truc profcssional.

Include in every contract and agreement a paragraph that communicates the *client's* responsibilities and obligations. Everything that you depend upon—from timely payment of invoices to the provision of documents, working space, and secretarial support—should be included.

122. Don't Try to Limit Your Liability

Trying to limit your liability in a contract may not always work. Courts may throw out the clause. And, saying you won't be held liable for your performance can hurt your chances of getting the contract in the first place. We all try to shift risk to others, but doing so makes us less desirable and attractive. Why should a client be willing to pay top dollar for a professional who is unwilling to take responsibility? Put yourself in the position of the client to determine what risks are reasonable for each party to assume.

123. Ask Your Clients to Pay in Advance

"In the Fortune 500 we trust; all others pay cash in advance." You can, if you wish, collect part or all of your fee in advance. Insist upon it. Look your clients coldly in the eye, hat brim to hat brim, boot toe to boot toe, in the middle of the town square at high noon. Tell them no work can be done on their behalf until a retainer in the amount of *X* dollars is advanced.

Then shut up! The next person to speak loses. If clients perceive that getting the contract is more important to you than the terms and conditions of payment, you will never get an advance retainer. If, however, clients recognize that the advance retainer is *an absolute requirement* for doing business with you, they will comply.

124. Handle Contracts and Collections with Reasonable Exactness

Approach the business side of your dealings with clients—contracts and collections—in an exacting but reasonable fashion. Well-written contracts that are as protective or more so of your *client's* interests than of yours are *essential* to generating referrals.

Should fee collection be necessary, it should be strong and professional, but *not* unduly intimidating. While there may be some immediate ill will, you should work to create an environment of long-term *respect* for business tactics necessary to protect your interests.

125. Find Someone to Play the Role of "Bad Guy"

In business, it sometimes becomes necessary to play a "bad guy" role. This may be required to collect fees, insist on providing services in a particular fashion, turn down business, or end a relationship with a client. Whenever possible, try to separate the bad guy role from the good guy impression by having these unpleasant tasks handled by a third party. If you have a partner, associate, or assistant, it is probably in your interest to let that person play the bad guy role for you and vice versa. This exchange allows you to extricate yourself while limiting the negative impact on future referral opportunities.

Chapter 10

Setting Professional Fees

126. Quote Fees on a Fixed-Price Basis

Quote your fee as a fixed price rather than on an hourly or daily basis, whenever possible. Your clients will find fixed fees more acceptable and you will be more profitable. Those professionals willing to work on a fixed-fee or fixed-price basis can enjoy a higher income than those who are only willing to work for an hourly or daily rate.

Most professionals fear taking a risk. But, increasingly, clients are just as fearful. Really, being in business means that you are willing to take risks. Doing so pays off! To make fixed fees profitable for you, however, you must master the skill of *estimating*.

If you quote fees on a fixed-price basis, always quote an unrounded number, preferably an odd number rather than even. Say the fee will be $3,980 rather than $4,000. The odd number gives the impression that you really used a sharp pencil, eliminating all possible fat.

If you feel that the potential client is a little hesitant about the fee, you may suggest an installment plan. Payments spread over the period of initial contact to the end of the project do not appear as overwhelming to some clients. Use your own discretion in handling this situation.

127. Set Fees Based on *Value,* not Time Spent

Establish fees that are based on the *value* of the services you've provided, not on the time spent on the project. Clients judge the wisdom of using your services based on their own agenda. They want to know if your services will help solve a problem, or if using your services will benefit them equal to or more than the cost of your services. Your fees must reflect value to the client.

You must also be willing to estimate the total time needed to get the job done when you are quoting fees on a time and materials basis. Just telling the client that you charge $125 an hour is not sufficient. The client needs to know the approximate or total number of hours you will take to produce the desired result.

128. Don't Pad Your Expense Account if Your Client is Paying

Oftentimes your work as a speaker, consultant, or specialist will require travel and related out-of-pocket expenses, such as meals, hotel, or car rentals. And often, your client contract or professional agreement will include a fee plus these costs. In other words, your client will expect to be billed for your out-of-pocket expenses.

When billing such incurred expenses, adopt this rule; never, never, *never* use your expense account as a profit center.

For example, let's assume standard airfare to your client's location is $800. But by buying early, you book the reservation at $550. Then are you obligated to pass along the savings to your client? Why not pad it to $800 and pocket the difference? Here's why: Being honest with your clients will pay long-term dividends. Collect for what you spend, but not a cent more. There will come a day when a client discovers that you are loading the expense account. You could destroy your professional reputation. How much is that worth?

129. Charge for Travel on a Per-Diem Basis

Frequently it is better to charge for travel expenses (hotel, meals, incidentals) on a per-diem basis rather than a direct reimbursement basis. Most clients prefer the simplicity of per-diem expenses and this arrangement avoids any criticism about how you spend expense dollars.

Think about having multiple per-diem rates—one for large, expensive cities and the other for smaller, inexpensive places. Set per-diem rates and define the quality of your life on the road in a way that is consistent with the style and expense that your client feels is appropriate. People are most comfortable when you do things the way *they* do them.

130. Don't Nickel and Dime Your Clients

Do not quote fees or invoice for services in a fashion that communicates that you are in any way petty or not delivering solid benefits for services provided. Almost all clients would prefer to pay a little more per hour or per day than to be burdened by many small charges for support services, activities, or costs that they feel should be included in the already high fee they are paying. A feeling that fees are *reasonable* and *predictable* and that invoices are not full of "nickel and dime" surprises will encourage referrals and future direct business.

131. Get Something Back When You Give Away Freebies

As a successful consultant and professional, you will frequently be asked for little favors, and since you can rarely collect for them, we term them "freebies."

These freebies can include everything from answering a quick question by phone to sending out copies of articles and documents. The list is endless. Now these free services can be turned into a profit center for you with the "one-minute commercial." Here's how.

When asked for a freebie or favor, quickly respond with one of these answers:

- "I'll take care of you . . . if you'll make me a deal."
- "I'll help if you make an agreement with me."
- "It is free . . . but there is a catch."
- "I can help you . . . but you must make me a promise."

And what is the deal, agreement, catch or promise you require of the person asking a freebie? It is simple . . . They simply promise, agree, or make you a deal to *call you first* when they need the services you provide. Add spice to your one-minute commercial by also getting them to promise or agree to recommend you to others.

The one-minute commercial can be fun for both parties, and a powerful sales tool for you.

Bonus tip: Use this technique *only* when you have done something free or extra for a prospect or client.

132. Consider Charging Clients for the Initial Session

When dealing with small, somewhat impoverished clients, it is usually in your interest to charge a fee (even if small) for the initial consultation. This fee will rid your marketing hours from time wasters who are unable to afford you fee. For many clients, the advice they obtain during the first half-hour or hour meeting may be sufficient for their needs.

Such a strategy may not be a good idea when dealing with large, well-financed prospects, however. Most often, they are not in need of or seeking free advice; instead, larger clients are usually interested in results over the long haul.

Don't hesitate to charge for diagnostic and needs-analysis services. Figuring out what the problem is may be the most valuable service you provide. Giving the answer away for free in the hope of getting an opportunity to implement your solution is poor marketing.

133. Cushion Fee Increases with a Benefit

When raising fees, be sure to provide a benefit to existing clients or prospects that you are currently marketing. Think about sending a letter indicating that fees will be raised on a specific date, but for existing clients or active prospects, fees will be raised at a later date. Or, indicate that any business committed by these people before a given date will be honored at the existing (lower) fee.

Don't raise your fees too often. Increase them by an amount sufficient to avoid raising them too often. Consider a period of a year or so.

In long-term contracts, protect your interests by including a cost-of-living clause to maintain your income should inflation become significant.

Communicate payment terms in the contract or agreement with your client; don't just leave it to trade custom. When money becomes tight, 30 days often becomes 60 or 90 days. Spell out the terms and conditions for payment in the agreement. While it does not ensure compliance, it does help you to collect fees due in a more timely fashion.

134. Don't Jump at the Opportunity to Cut Your Fee

Do not accept a request for a reduction in your fee unless the client is willing to accept a reduction in the scope of work. Bargaining makes you less desirable and creates the wrong image. If you communicate a willingness to accept less, you are letting the client know that either you are hungry and desperate or that your initial fee was inflated.

Some clients are not happy (and may not do business) unless they can drive a bargain. In such cases, again, cut your fee in exchange for a reduction in time and resources provided. This approach allows you to save face and permits the client to get the deal being sought.

Be especially cautious and reject offers to cut your fee or to provide services because of the "exposure" and "potentially beneficial contacts" you will receive from the project. You can't take potentials to the bank—and you will get exposure when you charge a fee. Think: When is the last time doctors, dentists, or attornies reduced *their* fees? Set a fair and justified professional fee and *stick to it*.

CHAPTER 11

Handling Client Concerns

135. *Be Prepared* to Answer Prospects' Questions and to Sell Your Services

"Be prepared," the old Boy Scout motto, fits this important marketing strategy. When making contact with prospects, there are three key questions everyone (you and all your staff) must be able to answer *quickly, confidentially* and *distinctly.*

A prospect wants to know:

1. *"Why should I listen to you?"*

   In other words, "what sets *you* apart from everyone else that would benefit me enough to give you my time and listen to your pitch?"
2. *"What's In It For Me?"*

   Your prospects want to know how what *you* do will make them more successful, more wealthy, more productive, work less, and so on. Avoid your selfish motives and focus on helping *them.*
3. *"Why should I use your services now?"*

   This question is the toughest of the three . . . how to motivate clients to take action *now.* Work to entice people to act instead of putting you off.

Bonus tip: If you have staff talking to prospects, make sure everyone is "singing from the same hymnal" when answering these three questions. Where appropriate, *script* your reply. Hold discussion and role-playing sessions with your staff. You may only get *one chance* to answer a prospect's three questions.

136. Lay a Client's Fears to Rest before Beginning Work on the Project

Be sure to identify the fears that prospective clients have about working with you. It takes some effort, but they will be reluctant to use your services until you have:

- Identified their fears.
- Discussed their fears.
- Laid their fears to rest.

For example, one of the greatest fears that clients have relates to your ability to produce the desired result on a *timely* basis. Always provide the prospective client with a schedule that identifies, with precision, *when* the various elements of your work will be completed. The schedule may change once work is underway, but it serves as a reassurance to your client that you have concern for their most important priority—*timely completion* of the project.

137. Make the Client See You as a Source of Value, Not a Threat

Do not accept business from clients who don't value your services or with whom you have personality conflicts. These clients will create more problems in the end, no matter how badly you need the business.

When working with the client's staff, you will probably be perceived as a threat. Reduce the degree of the threat by making the client properly introduce you and explain your role. Further reduce threat by communicating the fact that you want to work *with* the staff, not at their expense. Consider starting out with a small seminar to the staff to ease the tension and motivate them by showing how their role will benefit them as well as the company.

Your continued success will depend on your ability to bury your ego and let the key players in the client's organization get recognition for your accomplishments. Those who are important to future business and referrals will know that you are responsible for these achievements.

Don't allow your relationship with a client to deteriorate into one which is adversarial in nature. Your role is to serve the client first and only. Keep lines of communication open and honest. If they do deteriorate, stop providing services until the communications are patched.

Always be viewed by your clients as giving at least 110%. Give them extra value. You benefit by having others hold the perception that you will always give them more than expected.

138. Let Clients Know You Will Make Them Self-Sufficient

People are often reluctant to become your client or to refer business when they perceive that it will be a long-term expensive involvement. Increase the potential of gaining their business by taking the time to communicate that one of your operating philosophies is to train them to be self-sufficient. They need to know that the process is to make them self-reliant and to free them from the need to obtain desired results by continued involvement with outside sources.

Index